The Confessions of a Failed Perfectionist

How to get over self-hate, self-sabotage and feeling like a failure

By Stephanie Wood Miller

Published in the United States by Windyfoot Publishing
1146 North Central Avenue 312 Glendale, CA 91202

10 9 8 7 6 5 4 3 2 1
Printed in the United States of America

LIBRARY OF CONGRESS CATALOGING-IN-PUBLISHING DATA Miller, Stephanie Wood. The Confessions of a Failed Perfectionist: How to get over self-hate, self-sabotage and feeling like a failure

ISBN-13:
978-0692073148 (Windyfoot Publishing)

ISBN-10:
0692073140

To purchase this book please visit **TheLoveMandala.com** or **StephanieMillerArtist.com**

Dedicated everyone who
helped me recover

Also by Stephanie Miller
Derby Poems
The Wisdom of the Kitchen Manifesto
The Fabled Land

Contents

Part One

The Inelegant Failure of a Well-Intentioned Good Girl and The Shame That Followed

Part Two

Simple Tools to Help Deal with the Complicated Mess Known as Life

Part One
The Inelegant Failure of a Well-Intentioned Good Girl and The Shame That Followed

Why It's Okay That This Book is Riddled with Errors

Do you feel that you don't measure up? Do you feel like you are a fake and you'll be caught at any moment? Are you frustrated at yourself when make mistakes? If so, I know exactly how you feel. It's okay to make mistakes, that is what this whole book is about, but, if you're anything like me, you don't believe that's true. I wrote this book at the urging of my friend Martine. She asked me, "What is the one thing you have to do before you die?" I answered instantly, "Pass on what I've learned about recovering from shame." She said, "So write a book." And I did. That was almost four years ago, and I've finally finished. In true perfectionist style, I wrote it in about two months and then deliberated about it for three years. The book I have written is based on my own experience. I'm not a research scientist or a psychologist. I simply want to share what I've learned in the hope that it will help you. If any of it doesn't ring true, or doesn't help you, skip it and take only the parts that help.

I suffered from eating disorders and addictive behavior and I wrote this book from that perspective. I haven't really covered important topics like racism, gender identity, and sexual violence because these things are not part of my story. All of them are important topics that have been covered by people who are qualified to talk about their experience. I have included resources at the back of the book that I hope will be helpful.

Since you may be a perfectionist I should warn you, this book has errors in it. I decided it is complete *with its imperfections.* I deliberated about hiring a professional editor and decided not to. There are commas missing or misplaced. There may be misspellings. This isn't because I'm lazy or don't care, I have never cared about any project as much as I care about this. I want to share what I've learned with as many people as possible. I decided to release this book just as it is to give myself (and ultimately you) an opportunity to notice how it feels to do something imperfectly. I wrote a book. I didn't do it perfectly and then I published it. I hope you will find it a helpful example of allowing imperfection, because I'm pretty uncomfortable. I invite you to notice how you feel when you find an error. Pause and really look at your thoughts, then ask yourself = *How does it serve me to think this way?* If you find the errors annoying or unhelpful let me know, maybe I'll edit the next edition. Or maybe it's perfect just as it is.

The Adventures of a Self-Made Perfectionist

I have a picture of myself when I'm around three years old, wearing a black velvet jumper, white socks and black patent leather Mary Jane shoes. The most striking thing about this photo is how confident I look. I'm a happy child, clearly pleased with who I am and how I look. I was so young I don't remember that day or the confident, happy feeling. It is safe to say that even today it is an unfamiliar feeling. The feeling of being an imposter, of not measuring up, of failing and of self-hatred has occupied the vast majority my life.

I had every good reason to be happy as a child. Growing up in Southern California life wasn't difficult. I was the firstborn daughter and the only grandchild on both sides of my family. My father worked and went to school while my mother stayed home and raised me and eventually my sister who I adored.

This is the abiding mystery of shame. Where does it come from and why does it happen? I believe shame grows like weeds. The seeds are present in everyone if they are nurtured, or, more accurately, if the tools of a healthy self-image aren't implemented. As Dr. Brene Brown says, shame is the fear that we are not worthy of belonging[1]. In modern society, the opportunity to feel like we don't belong has exploded exponentially with the advent of social media. In human society, it can happen anywhere. The dark interior sense of being insufficient can spring up in almost any environment rich, poor, happy, disappointing or abusive. It helps to think of shame as a dis-ease that can happen to anyone, not as an affliction particular to you or your children as a result of some failure. The good news is, it is possible to recover given careful cultivation of some tools and the willingness to change. I share my experience because I think it is helpful and believe it helps to discover we are not alone.

As I child I felt a tremendous sense of responsibility for the feelings and the well-being of everyone around me. When my mother was unhappy I thought it was my fault. When my sister skinned her knee, I felt I should have prevented it. If my dad was angry I thought it was because I was a bad girl. I spent much of my childhood trying and failing to control the messy, unpredictable world around me. This chronic failure to keep people from feeling pain or crying, objects from getting lost or broken, or accidents from happening led to a deep belief

---

[1] *Daring Greatly: How the Courage to Be Vulnerable Transforms the Way We Live, Love, Parent, and Lead* by Brene Brown © 2015

that I was not enough. I became convinced that I didn't make mistakes but that I actually WAS a mistake. Feeling like a mistake, instead of feeling like a healthy, whole human being *who occasionally made mistakes,* was the beachhead of a life-long struggle with shame. It would be many years before I was introduced to the Buddhist concept of samsara which acknowledges the reality that life is a cycle of birth, suffering, death and rebirth. If I had known this when I was young, I might not have experienced so much unhappiness trying to combat this simple truth.

I was prone to a kind of obsessive thinking that caused me to review events over and over in my mind. No matter how much I reviewed events in my life, I always came to a negative conclusion. I believed I had done something wrong and that something else bad was about to happen.

My sense of dread and anxiety was augmented by being a child in the 60's. Daily news of death toll in Vietnam, the Soviet threat, acts of protest, violence and assassinations poured out of the television in our living room. All these events contributed to a pervasive feeling that the world was going wrong and I needed to do something to put it right. The birth of the ecological preservation movement made me feel guilty and sorry for using up the earth's resources, and as an American, eating more than my fair share of the food.

Around the time I turned 10, I began to engage in a battle with my body. For reasons I can't explain, I never wanted to be a girl. I felt that being a girl was second class. I felt betrayed by a body that wasn't as strong or as fast as a boy's body. I felt that if I could be a boy I could do the things I really wanted to do like be a pro baseball pitcher or an astronaut. This was at the dawn of feminism when women seldom worked outside the home or had the opportunity to do the things that men did. Society changed, but the inside of my head didn't. I still hated being a girl, not because I wanted to be a boy, but because I felt girls weren't good enough.

This battle would manifest as a life-long rejection of my femininity and a misguided mistrust of women and girls. I grew up in neighborhood that was primarily boys. I played three-flies-up, HORSE and one-on-one basketball with the boys in our local park. I was tall and fairly coordinated and I was able to keep up with them. More than once I was picked first to play on a boys' team but I never seemed to retain the positive message this implied. I only seemed to notice when I was picked last or I made a mistake. This was another habit that fostered shame and thwarted my self-esteem. I clung to the negative outcome or failure as a mark of my irreparable wrongness. I hadn't learned to weigh good and bad outcomes equally.

In my early teen years, my dad took up jogging. At the time this was unusual. People didn't run for daily exercise, nor were gyms a part of people's everyday life. Daily exercise was for pro-athletes and Olympians. Around this same time my mom went on a diet using a well-known program. As a result of my dad exercising and my mom dieting, I came up with the idea that the key to being good enough was to be thin. So, for the next thirty years, I yo-yoed back and forth between my parents two examples exercising on the one hand and dieting on the other.

Over the years following childhood I engaged in endless cycles of dieting, bingeing, starving and exercising in order to achieve the perfect weight. I don't blame my parents for this behavior because I know they were trying to take care of their health. It was my unhealthy response to their normal behavior that caused the problem. The irony was that, like so many aspects of my life, I could never achieve perfection. Wherever I set the bar I always found myself falling slightly short. The cruelty of perfectionism is that we constantly move the finish line. We set out for one goal and when we achieve it or get close, we move the goal further away. It never occurred to me that my standards were completely subjective and therefore meaningless.

Things got worse when I reached puberty. My body, which I already mistrusted, betrayed me further by shooting up 6" in one year and then developing hips and breasts. I looked less and less like a boy and felt awkward and uncomfortable wherever I went. My once silky, straight hair turned curly, frizzy and unmanageable. What I saw when I looked in the mirror (however inaccurate) was a disaster and it fostered a new level of self-hatred. My body was just one more thing I couldn't control in my litany of failures. While other girls were starting to think about boys or developing a natural curiosity about sex. I was terrified by the idea of kissing a boy or anyone seeing my feminine body naked. The idea of that kind of intimacy made me feel feverish with anxiety. I developed a habit of prudishness and intentionally avoided even talking to my peers about sex or any kind of feminine maturity. I dated a little in high school, but I ran away in terror at the first sign of a boy liking me or wanting any kind of genuine intimacy.

I carried on this way until I got to college where I fell in love with an older student for the first time in my life. At the time, he seemed mature and worldly. I was so flattered by his attention I barely noticed as he gradually took control on my life. Because of my well-developed sense of shame and inadequacy, I accepted his controlling, abusive behavior as what I deserved. The idea that I should be cherished or respected was a remote concept. This part of my life has given me genuine empathy for women trapped in abusive relationships. The cycle of feeling unworthy, longing for love and be willing to sacrifice self-respect to get it is a hellish Catch 22 that too many women succumb to. At the base of this dangerous dynamic is shame, silently rendering women helpless to save themselves until, for many, it's too late.

When I entered the work force I discovered a whole new realm of shame and perfectionism. In the work place my perceived failures were now measured by more tangible things, such as dollars, promotions, and opportunities. No matter how I succeeded, I could always point to a peer or a friend who was doing better or who had succeeded a little bit more. This added a new dimension to my feeling of shame. I began to worry about being an imposter. I worked in advertising for many years but no matter how much experience I acquired I always felt that I wasn't a real _____. I feared being caught, that someone would realize that I was really an outsider who had conned my way into an advertising job. This, of course, bore to little relationship to reality. During most of my career I worked as a freelancer which meant I was always hired based on my skills. The fact that I was hired and recommended by the same people again and again never seemed to alleviate my feeling of being an imposter.

There were, of course, people and circumstances that contributed to the development of my pervasive sense of failure and lack, but ultimately

I believe most of the problem was inside my head. I adopted a way of thinking and reacting that cultivated the weeds of shame. They sprung up, matured and re-seeded themselves until I was ready to change.

I will tell you what I did to change and what I did to cultivate a healthy mindset, but first I want to talk about some of the components of perfectionism and shame. Understanding the problem, as well as seeing some of the common behaviors, may help with your recovery from perfectionism and shame.

Monday Morning and The Silver Bullet

I have always engaged in perfectionist thinking. The important thing about being a perfectionist is not that I am perfect, but that I think that I should be. Being a perfectionist is buying into the idea that it is possible to avoid making mistakes. Perfectionism is the idea that life has a finish line and that I should cross it first. In retrospect, it isn't surprising that I joined the track team. A foot race is the most appealing competition possible to a perfectionist. There's a beginning and an end and a clear winner. Thirty years after my last race I still revel in the feeling of winning. There is a pure fulfillment of being the best by some objective standard. However, life is very seldom like a 200 -meter sprint. There are hundreds of ways to do things, all of them potentially 'the right way.' Winning in life has no guarantee of any reward. However, I have always longed for some objective standard that I could achieve. I have always wanted there to be a way to do things without any errors. This kind of thinking goes way beyond any normal competition like a tennis match or a card game. Whatever the circumstance, I don't necessarily want to win I just want to be perfect.

Monday Morning

I applied this relentless perfectionism to my body for years. I obsessed about the idea that my hips were too square and my thighs were too long. I scrutinized my body looking for the flaws that made me less than perfect. One area of relentless perfectionism was the pursuit of the perfect weight. The thing about being a perfectionist is that whenever I approached my goal I moved the finish line. *I'll be perfect when I weigh 142 pounds...Well actually 138 pounds...Okay, now I think I should weigh 134 pounds.* And on and on.

I felt the same way about my every aspect in my life. *I'll be perfect when I am married...I'll be perfect when I get this job... I'll be perfect when I buy this house.*

This way of thinking fueled an endless cycle and I always feeling I had come up a little short. In my experience, nothing fuels shame more effectively than perfectionism.

With my weight, as with many other conditions in my life, I always fixated on some distant day when I would start diet or a new exercise program. This is what I call Monday Morning Thinking. *Starting Monday, I will do this perfectly.*

This inevitably led to bingeing on Sunday

afternoon before the new diet started. It was my way of counterbalancing the coming 'perfection.' That story always ended the same way. After a while, I grew tired of trying to eat perfectly or not achieving the desired effect with my exercise goals, and quit. This led to another round of shame, followed by a new Monday Morning. I repeated this cycle so many times I became exhausted by my own insanity.

I was never very good at moderation. I tended to go all in most of the time. I saw things as black-and-white. When one of my girlfriends said, "Is there a third alternative?" I remember being shocked by the realization that the world was more than pass or fail. This kind of black-an-white thinking was detrimental in many of the situations I faced in my adult life.

There are no winners and losers in friendships and marriages. Most days at work are characterized by degrees of completion and success. In fact, very few situations in life really can be experienced in black-and-white. The vast majority of experiences are various shades of gray. As this realization began to sink in my perfectionism began to lose its strangle hold on me. *If there is no clear, perfect conclusion then I can't do it perfectly.* Gradually, I've been able to begin let go of Monday Morning Thinking and find ways to make minor improvements in the present. If I'm unhappy with my weight, I can cut back on salt, I don't need to start a new diet. If

I'm tired of being late for work, I can get up five minutes earlier tomorrow and see if that helps. I've found that simple small changes are much more effective than giant sweeping Monday Morning plans. I've even begun to boycott New Year's resolutions. I don't have to wait until the beginning of the year to make a change, I start right now.

Silver Bullet Thinking

As a perfectionist, I was always looking for the once and for all solution. To this day, it irks me that so much of life is repetitive. I want the kitchen to stay perpetually clean. I want bills to stay paid. I want the gas tank to stay full. Every time these things are done I feel a tremendous sense of satisfaction and security. Yet as the days go along, dirty dishes accumulate, new bills arrive and the gas tank empties out and I'm perpetually annoyed that I have to do it all again. As a recovering perfectionist, the daily-ness of life is annoying to me. This is because somewhere in my mind I think things should get fixed and stay fixed. The underlying thinking is viewing these things as problems instead of recognizing that life involves repetitious activities. The reality that I need another shower isn't a problem, it's just part of being human.

My idea that I can solve these problems once and for all is what I call Silver Bullet Thinking. I want to find a way to solve whatever I perceive as a problem once and for all. I want to put a bullet in the heart of the problem and put an end to it forever. Diffusing Silver Bullet Thinking begins by recognizing that life experiences are not a problem. Doing laundry, buying groceries, figuring out what to eat for lunch are not problems, they are simply a part of living in modern society.

I have to give up the idea of my own personal omnipotence. No matter how badly I may want to do something it may not be possible. I genuinely believe I have a better idea for how the US Government should be run but I'm not the dictator of the US and I don't get to decide. I need to recognize my own sense of powerlessness to change the current situation. This is not to say that I can't try to make things better. Everything I do can be motivated by a sense of compassion and service. What isn't healthy for me is the idea that I can fix everything and it will *stay fixed*. Recognizing the vagaries of life makes it possible to face life with more serenity and grace. Acknowledging my position on the planet helps me to see things calmly and clearly. There is nothing particularly wrong, nothing that needs to be fixed, nothing that is forever. I can relax and give the perfectionist a vacation.

I can't fix my perfectionism overnight but I can recognize the ways it manifests in my life and try not to act on it. I try, whenever I catch myself, not to engage in Monday Mornings Thinking or using Silver Bullets.

The Tyranny of Should

The demon spawn of perfectionism is Should. The use, or I *should* say, overuse of this word is virtually epidemic. Should is the agent of perfectionism. It implies that there is some objective external standard for what you do or what you are. It creeps into our thoughts and our language every day and is seldom productive. This word precludes the possibility that I am human, prone to mistakes, liable to do something less than perfectly. Most of the time when I say *should* I am using it as a weapon against myself. *I should go on a diet. I should have called her back sooner. I should have thought of that.*

Should is like a shadow cast across your life every day. When I say, "*I should*" I'm suggesting that I'm incomplete, that I need to do something else to be whole. Part of recovering from eating disorders was coming to the realization that I'm already whole. I'm complete and perfect just as I am right now, not five pounds from now. It also means that I don't need to attend parties, cover the gray in my hair or pick-up a friend at the airport to be a better person. I do all of these things, but not because I *should*.

I was telling a friend about a mistake I made at work. I said, "I should have known better." She said, "How would you have known better? Has it happened before?" I realized she was right, that any time I made a mistake I immediately assume that it was in my I should have known better even when I had no experience. My friend had a wonderful and useful philosophy that is applicable to the use of the word Should. She says that we made up a set of rules about the way the world works, the trouble is that many of us made up these rules when we were four-year-olds. My four-year-old made up many arbitrary rules about what I and others should be doing. At such a young age, with so little life experience, these rules are at best simplistic, and at worst, detrimental to functioning as an adult in the world.

I often say that if I was put in an operating room and told to perform neurosurgery I would think "I *should* know how to do this." It sounds ludicrous but that's how I think. I assume that I should be able to master a skill simply because there is a need. This isn't pride its shame. It is the pervasive sense that if I can't master everything I'm a failure. A great acronym for SHAME is **S**hould **H**ave **A**lready **M**astered **E**verything.

When I catch myself thinking that I should be able to master something I've never done or that I should have foreseen an unfavorable outcome,

I just remind myself that a four-year-old made the rules. The adult I am now is better informed and better able to assess my success or failure in any given situation.

Notice the "Shhh" sound at the beginning of the word Should. Often we use the word, "Should' against ourselves to silence our hopes and dreams or to dampen our enthusiasm. "I'd like to write a book, but I *sh*ould get a paying job." Using this word can also feel painful when you use it on others, because you may be silencing them as well.

There are a few instances when "should" can be used without harm, as in 'I should pay my taxes.' But these instances are rare and avoiding the use of the word can be a revelation. Part Two of this book includes some guidance on managing "Should."

The Worldwide Conspiracy Against Me

Life is hard and messy. Everyone faces disappointment, gets sick, loses loved ones and ages. We would all like to believe that our story is unique, but the truth is, for most of us, our story is the human story. Most us have some good fortune and some suffering and, were we able to quantify it, we would probably find out that life doles out good fortune and bad fortune about equally. For some people, people who think like me, we adopt a faulty system of rating life's ups and downs. We give extra weight to negative events and undervalue positive ones. Slowly we begin to develop a story that goes like this: *This always happens to me. Things always go wrong. I'm unlucky.*

The striking thing about this kind of thinking is how small it is. How narrowly it focuses on me and my world and what happens to me. We descend into a habit of being a victim. We begin to believe the story that we tell ourselves over and over. We believe we are powerless. We believe that circumstances and people are working against us and before long we see ourselves trapped in a conspiracy that is constantly trying to defeat our true desires. For years, I said, somewhat ironically, "The world is in a conspiracy against me." I said it because on some level I really did believe that the traffic that made me late, or the penalty for late payment on a credit card, were the result of a conspiracy – not the actual consequence of my own actions. Consequences I might add, that were handed out without prejudice to anyone in the same circumstance.

This is lie of victimhood, *I'm being singled out. Bad things only happen to me. I'm the only one.* It simply isn't true. Most misfortunes in life are handed out equally. People in every stratum of society suffer from cancer, experience personal set-backs, have to sit in traffic or lose someone or something they love.

There is a powerful narrative in our culture that creates and perpetuates the victim myth. We believe in an interdependent relationship of the victim, the perpetrator and the rescuer[2]. We have an entire belief system predicated on disempowering us and waiting for a magical rescuer. This paradigm can be seen in our fairy tales, myths and movies. The problem with this is that it allows, and possibly even encourages, a lack of personal responsibility. If we are perpetually stuck blaming circumstances and other people we won't awaken to our own personal power.

---

[2] See the work of Fleet Maull and his concept of Radical Responsibility®.

We all know stories of people who found themselves in the role of victim and decided not to accept it. We are almost always inspired by these stories in part because we love hearing about someone who has overcome an obstacle. We all love to see the victim transformed into a survivor. The irony for many of us is, we are erecting our own obstacles with the way we think. Almost everything we encounter presents us with a choice. We can choose to be a victim or we can choose to accept circumstances as a part of life. Freedom from thinking like a victim will only come once we acknowledge we have been thinking like a victim and start trying to think differently.

One of the most inexplicable stories in the Bible is the story of Job who was favored by God and lived a life of good fortune. Then God, in what seems reminiscent of Randolph and Mortimer Bellamy in Trading Places, allows Job to be tested. He loses his home, family and livelihood. I think the point of the story is the ineffable truth that we don't necessary receive what we earn and that our goodness or badness is not a determinant of our success or wealth. It is a truth we all have to wrestle with: Why do bad things happen? And why do they happen to *me*?

The new testament includes an equally disconcerting truth where Jesus says, "But I say to you, love your enemies, bless those who curse you, do good to those who hate you, and pray for those who spitefully use you and persecute you, that you may be sons of your Father in heaven; for He makes His sun rise on the evil and on the good, and sends rain on the just and on the unjust[3]." He speaks to the reality that it rains on everyone and it doesn't have anything to do with reward or punishment.

Victimhood has two powerful allies. The first is terminal uniqueness. This is the idea that somehow my case is genuinely special. It is a habit, particularly in American society, to think of ourselves as the hero of our own movie. Of course, there is a degree of truth to this. We are, in fact, at the center of our own life but what we fail to recognize is that our story isn't that unique is the sweep of human history. Millions of us have walked the planet and experienced life on earth, our character and our story is not new. Even people who are famous, rich or extraordinary aren't really that special. Do you know who Gil Eannes, Paavo Nurmi or Sybil Ludington are? All of them were once famous people now lost is the flow of history. Five hundred years from now a school child may not be able to say who Albert Einstein was or what Abraham Lincoln did. The recognition that we are neither particularly unique nor that our role in history unimportant can come as a

---

[3] Matthew 5:45

tremendous relief. It's great to play the hero of your story, be honorable, treat others with respect and compassion, leave behind an admirable story, just have a proper sense of the size and sweep of world history. The point is not to exaggerate the importance of your own story.

Victimhood's other boon companion is self-pity. For years, I cultivated my self-pity gradually adding stories to the narrative. I kept a record in my head of the ways in which I had been wronged by individuals and institutions. I treated it like a rare pet that needed constant attention. Over time it grew fat and demanding. I had to fuel my self-pity with false stories and even reshape the events of my life to match my narrative. I also maintained a circle of people who would support my story and my self-pity. I moved away from relationships in which someone encouraged me to take responsibility for my own actions or questioned my version of events. All of this was exhausting to maintain, but I became comfortable being a victim and unwilling to adopt a different perspective.

Being a victim was a natural talent for me. I wasn't encouraged to feel sorry for myself, nor did I have a particularly difficult life. It was mostly that I felt being a victim was a good way to get more love and attention. I'm still prone to slide into victimhood when things don't go my way.

I'm able to see myself with more compassion now. Because I didn't experience what I felt was enough love and attention I used victimhood to get more of what I felt I needed. It was a flawed strategy, but I was young when I started doing it. From that vantage point I'm able to see myself with greater compassion and extend that compassion to others.

The Illusion of Control

When my mom was ill I spent months navigating through the labyrinth of hospitals, specialists and insurance companies. I spent hours talking to doctors trying to understand the science behind different medical solutions and almost as much time trying to understand hospital policies and staffing. Along the way I made hundreds of decisions from whether or not she wanted to be propped up to whether we should pursue a different course of treatment. Despite the fact that I applied every ounce of energy, effort and intelligence I had to my mother's well-being, she still died. My first reaction was to feel like a failure.

I found myself going over and over the decisions I had made over the past months. I replayed scenarios over in my head speculating on a different outcome. When I joined a grief support group I expressed my feelings of guilt and failure about my mom's death. The gentle facilitator of our group pointed out that guilt is our attempt to make believe that we're able to control something that is both uncontrollable and incomprehensible. It took me months to realize that no matter how desperately I wanted to keep my mom alive, I was never responsible for her death.

My husband later pointed out that I had crafted a

narrative in which I had sole responsibility for my mom's well-being. In fact, I have a step-father and 5 siblings and we consulted at least 20 medical specialists. We made all the decisions about my mom's care as a team and my mom was the final arbiter of what she was willing and unwilling to do.

This is the funny thing about the illusion of control, it immediately isolates us from others. I think I, and I alone, have to figure things out and solve the problem. I think when things go wrong it's my fault. If I dig under the surface of this idea there's an ugly truth: I think I have an extraordinary amount of power to influence and change things. My sense of my own importance in any situation is inflated beyond what is humanly possible. The beautiful, heart-breaking truth is that all of life is interconnected and none of us are ever alone. Even in the blackest moment of despair what is happening to me is happening to someone else and the events swirling around me are part of a massive cosmic stew that is impossible for me to comprehend.

An exaggerated sense of my personal power and self-reliance, contrary to conventional wisdom, generates fear and anxiety. The belief that I'm in-control, or may presently achieve control is a road to insanity. No amount of intelligence or power makes it possible for me to keep the earth spinning on its axis. Shantideva an eighth-century Buddhist monk taught a very simple principle that relates to this idea of control and worry.

If the problem can be solved why worry?

If the problem cannot be solved worrying will do you no good

A friend of mine once suggested I make a list of all the things I could control and all the things I couldn't. The first thing I listed that I could control was 'what I eat', then, after a moment of reflection I realized that wasn't really true. Sometimes I can't get what I want to eat, sometimes I don't have time to eat, and sometimes someone else decides what I'm going to eat. Then I wrote 'what time I go to bed', unless I get a phone call, or my neighbors has a loud party, or I have work to do. I started the list of what I can't control, which was much easier. I wrote 'sunrise, sunset, weather, natural disasters, terrorists, politics, airline schedules, traffic, mean people, the price of gasoline, the neighbor's barking dog, what my husband does...' The point being that most of the things that irritate me are out of control. Life is chaotic and the vast majority of things that happen to me are outside of my control.

At this point I just want to scream. "BUT I AM RESPONSIBLE!" So much of my identity is wrapped up in being a responsible adult, showing up on time and doing the right thing. It rocks my world to feel I am powerless over most of the events in my day. But, it's true, so I have to find a way to navigate through the thousands of things I can't control every day.

First, I have to practice acceptance. Recognizing that life is messy and accepting it is the only way forward. Whenever I try to grab the steering wheel and drive the truth is it's only an illusion. Most things aren't really controllable.

I find the sentiment of this ancient nursery rhyme to be helpful:

For every ailment under the sun

There is a remedy, or there is none;

If there be one, try to find it;

If there be none, never mind it.[4]

The prayer originally attributed to Reinhold Niebuhr[5] and popularized by the Alcoholics Anonymous movement as the Serenity Prayer also expresses this idea of acceptance:

God, grant me the serenity to accept the things I cannot change,

Courage to change the things I can,

---

[4] Mother Goose rhyme (1695)

[5] It is not known who originally wrote this prayer, it is most commonly attributed to Reinhold Niebuhr but there is evidence that he may not be the original author.

And the wisdom to know the difference.

I have found this useful to apply to many daily situations. I ask myself can I change this? If the answer is YES I try my best to do my part. If the answer is NO I try to let go and relax. It doesn't change the fact that I may experience guilt for something I haven't done or shame about something I have done but at least it gives me an opportunity *to try* and accept things exactly as they are.

Living in the Maids Quarters in the Hamptons

I was always slightly taller than most of my peers and I was sensitive about sticking out. When I was in third grade I was bullied into standing back-to-back with the tallest boy in the school. I remember him as an awkward, gawky social outcast and any comparison to him made me heartsick. There was something about this experience that degraded both of us. It turned out I was slightly taller and I was mortified. I didn't want to return to school the next day. I had the feeling that my body had betrayed me by growing taller and I couldn't control it. This may have been my first experience with the feeling of shame, the idea that my body was a mistake. In retrospect, the saddest thing about this experience was that I lacked compassion for myself and for this awkward boy who no doubt felt as badly as I did about being bullied.

In seventh grade, I grew six inches in one year. I went from being an inch or so taller than my peers to being a full head taller. I grew so quickly that I became unable to control my limbs or to gauge if I'd fit in a space. My body felt wildly out of control, which just seemed to grow and grow. I still remember walking down the hallway between classes looking over a sea of heads, all of them shorter than me. In retrospect, if you asked my classmates I don't think they'd remember me as being particularly tall, but I felt like a freak. I was already uncomfortable with being a girl and I dreaded starting my period, growing breasts and becoming a woman. I would reach middle age before I began to accept and embrace having curves and being feminine.

My most torturous experiences were the school dances. I remember waiting desperately for a boy who was confident enough or tall enough to ask me to dance. I mostly remember standing against the wall watching the other kids dance and fully understanding the meaning of the term 'wall flower'. To this day I remember being asked to dance by a boy named Scott who must have 6 or 7 inches shorter than me. He walked over with a confident swagger and escorted me to the floor. I felt like an idiot since I had hardly ever danced with a boy and I was so much taller. As I often did at that time in my life, I missed the positive message that a boy had asked me to dance and focused instead on my awkwardness.

This feeling of being big fueled my lifelong obsession with being thin. I thought if I couldn't be short at least I could make myself weigh less. My head became a petty tyrant subjecting my body to its unreasonable whims. It was during this time that I began to become estranged from my body. If it wouldn't cooperate with me (by which I meant the ideas in my head) then I wouldn't listen to it. When I hurt myself, I would ignore the pain. If I was hungry, I'd skip eating, harboring the false idea that I wouldn't grow into a woman if I didn't eat. I felt there was no one I could talk to. Adults always said things like, "You're so lucky to have the height" or, "Just wait until you are older you'll love being tall." I found this kind of encouragement ridiculous because all I wanted was to fit in, and I didn't care what happened when I was 20 which seemed like a lifetime away.

In high school, I started running track. This was the era of "no pain no gain" training. Coaches routinely told us to run through the pain and stop whining. Nothing could have appealed to me more. I was given permission to subjugate by body to the punishment it deserved. Unfortunately, the more pain I felt the more I succeeded resulting in the unhealthy idea of performance and its relationship to pain. I began to see joint pain, sore muscles and hunger as a necessary ingredient to athletic success. Like so many things in life, this is partially true, but I always had the idea that "if some is good then more is better". My body became nothing more than a whiny impediment to the goals my head made up. When I failed, I trained harder. I would give myself extra work-outs with the intention of hurting myself.

As I look back, I'm saddened by the way I

squandered my natural talent and caused my body permanent damage. I loved running, it made me feel free and happy. I continued punishing my body the same way for many years. Eventually, I did so much damage it became difficult for me to run at all.

Many years later I recognized how cruel I was to my body at this time in my life. I realized that I wasted years either warring with or ignoring my body. I finally realized that my body was more than the vehicle that carried my head around and that it actually is a source of life, energy and wisdom. I began to see that my connection to the earth and to others was through my body. I started to appreciate that my body knows as much or more than my head.

One simple but memorable experience happened when I returned home after a long trip in India. I had lost nearly 45 pounds and had eaten almost nothing for months. At the time, I wasn't in the habit of listening to my body. I was suffering from muscle cramps and headaches as a result of near starvation. I craved Caesar salad for weeks. I learned later that Caesar salad with anchovies is a source of calcium, magnesium, iron and potassium, all minerals that were severely depleted in my system. My body knew where to get what it needed, even though my head did not.

I've learned to ask my body what it needs and my

body almost always answers with a sensible request. Once I began working with my body instead of against it I found I experienced a profound sense of well-being. Now I understand that my body needs sleep, exercise and healthy food. I particularly notice mood swings when I eat poorly or don't get enough sleep.

My body is a source of innate, non-conceptual wisdom[6]. It doesn't have ideas it has feelings. By locating feelings in my body, I have been able to learn how to interpret my emotions.

My body is the source of intuition. My body is also able to identify bad situations more quickly than my head, it feels when things just aren't right. The more I listen to my body the more smoothly things seem to go. Some of the most bitter lessons of my life have come as a result of ignoring the feeling in my gut. Attending to a feeling of dizziness, nausea or back pain instead of pushing through has often yielded in unexpected, positive results.

---

[6] I found *Touching Enlightenment: Finding Realization in the Body* by Reginald A. Ray Ph.D. to be very illuminating on this subject.

After years of recovery, I finally recognize my body is like an amazing house in the Hamptons, spacious, beautiful, and full of resources. For years, I kept it locked up and lived in my head like a penniless maid. The discovery that I possess this extraordinary wealth has been like winning the lottery. I could move back to the maid's quarters anytime I want, but, why would I?

Good Girls Don't Cry

When I was young, my dad went to school in the daytime and worked nights. We were frequently told to keep quiet while he was sleeping. This became a metaphor for my emotional life. Like my voice, I was always trying to keep my emotions down. I had the idea that it wasn't okay to have feelings, particularly negative feelings. When I felt strong emotions I believed I had to hide them. It was part of my Good Girl syndrome. Good girls don't cause trouble, they don't make a scene, they don't make anyone uncomfortable. My desire to be a Good Girl went way beyond what was healthy, I wanted to be the Best Good Girl ever.

When I was about five years old I was awakened in the night by a terrible thunder storm, the first I had experienced in my lifetime. Thunderstorms are rare in Southern California and my parents had never explained them to me. I was terrified, I thought the world was coming to an end. I cowered in my bed feeling that I couldn't run into my parent's bedroom for comfort. I had to be tough, suck up my fear and not cause any trouble. In the morning, I didn't mention my terror and my parents didn't mention the storm so I felt that I had done the right thing by not running to them for comfort. Gradually, just as I had learned to ignore my body, I began to ignore my feelings. If I was angry I often made jokes or sarcastic remarks rather than address what was bothering me. It became a lifelong habit to sublimate my feelings.

Over time I began to adopt methods for numbing my feelings. The essential thing for me was to avoid feeling the sting of the actual emotion in the moment. I found food to be particularly effective and whenever I felt feelings, particularly big or unmanageable ones, I would retreat into a box of cookies, buttered toast, or a bag of chips. I also used exercise as a means for dulling my feelings, in college I would run for miles until I was too exhausted to feel anything.

One dictionary definition of numb is "deprived of the power to feel or move normally; emotionally unresponsive; indifferent[7]." This perfectly describes my emotional state. Over the years I became unable to respond normally to emotional situations. At work, I was always known for my steady temperament and for never losing my temper. In truth, advertising is an infuriating business fraught with almost constant stress from deadlines. The difficult personalities and the endless unreasonable client demands did make me angry but I ignored the emotions. I suffered

[7] The American Heritage Dictionary of the English Language

severe migraines, neck and back pain. Once I started acknowledging my true feelings in the moment many of my physical symptoms disappeared.

As time went on I could really only identify three distinct emotions, happy, unhappy and mad. The nuance of the emotional experience of being human was lost on me. I didn't distinguish between happy and excited or unhappy and anxious. I prided myself on being emotionally steady, logical and dependable. My friends and family turned to me for advice and I took this as sign of their approval.

Until I got into therapy I gave very little thought to how I actually felt about a situation. On the rare occasions I expressed strong emotions I always felt ashamed and apologetic afterwards. Later when a therapist asked me how I felt about a particular situation my most common response was "I don't know." This was an honest response, after 30 years of sublimating my feelings I could no longer feel or identify them. This led to a feeling of indifference towards the emotions of others since I was so out of touch with my emotions. It also caused me to feel isolated since the emotions of others were unfamiliar to me. I mostly felt they were overreacting. I considered most women to be overly dramatic, irrational and unreasonable. My ability to sympathize with people who were struggling was extremely limited.

As a card carrying Good Girl I am always uncomfortable with messiness. I still catch myself thinking a sink full of dishes is a moral failing. I constantly try to improve situations and offer (unsolicited) advice on how to do most everything. The childhood warning that "nobody likes a know-it-all" rings in my ears but I simply can't help feeling I know how things should be done. I'm genuinely afraid that if I don't correct something that looks wrong to me I'll be held accountable later. Only in recent years have I found the compassion to see myself as someone who fears disorder and is petrified of doing things wrong. My rigidity is an armor I wear to protect a vulnerable heart.

My therapist suggested that I try looking at my feelings by locating them in my body. It took a while but eventually I noticed where different emotions resided. As feelings welled up I would locate them in my body which helped identify and remove the numbness.

I was especially resistant to crying. Whenever I cried I felt ashamed, embarrassed and apologetic. If I was unable to avoid crying I would go someplace where I could cry privately. I viewed crying as a moral failing but also as a sign that I had done something wrong. If I had done everything right there would be no need to cry. I saw crying as a sign of weakness and failure.

My therapist suggested that I imagine my tears possessed a substance that came exclusively from crying and nourished my heart. This helped me to begin to see crying as a healthy act of self-care. I've come to believe that our cultural addiction to aggression has limited our ability to see our own vulnerability. All human beings have tender hearts, and in an effort to protect them, we often lose the ability to feel them. Permitting myself to cry has allowed me to witness others crying without judgment and to connect to others at a heart level.

Over the past several years I have been cultivating my own vulnerability, instead of rejecting the lump in my throat I explore it. Oddly enough I've discovered one of the things I cry about is seeing human strength. If I watch a group of people rescuing beached whales or helping someone after a natural disaster, I'll burst into tears. When I was finally willing to look at my own tears I saw that it was an appreciation of human power and ingenuity. Crying wasn't a sign of weakness, it was sign of appreciation, and a feeling of connection to others. Crying also led to an increased ability to feel the full gamut of my emotions. When I began to cry more I began to the emotions of others. The tears began to thaw my emotional numbness. I was surprised to discover Good Girls *do cry* and it makes them better human beings.

Especially Among Women

Shame has a universal quality and seems to affect both men and women. However, because I am a woman I wanted to talk about some of the qualities of shame that are particular to women. I don't believe it makes women's shame greater but I do think there are factors in our culture which contribute to the texture and severity of our experience of shame.

I believe that human society has lost its balance between masculine and feminine. I want to be completely clear that I am talking about *masculine* and *feminine* principals **not** men vs. women. It is true that men tend to behave in a masculine way and women in a feminine way and this is exactly my point. We all possess both masculine and feminine qualities. Watch a man hold a baby and you will see his feminine side. Watch a woman compete in a marathon and you will see her masculine qualities. At its simplest, the masculine principle produces action and the feminine principle produces space. It is expressed physically by the penetrating penis and the spacious womb.

Aggression and submission are the extreme form of these healthy qualities. The healthy form aggression is entering and healthy form of submission is allowing. These qualities could also be expressed as movement and stillness. In many cases, we are just overdoing these natural healthy aspects of our humanity. I don't believe women should take over the world nor do I believe fighting patriarchal norms in an aggressive way will solve the problem. The real problem is in each one of us when we deny, mask or sublimate the natural balance of masculine and feminine qualities inside of us.

Our glorification of physical strength is visible in who we consider heroes, athletes who hit hard on the field or behave violently off the field. We love movie characters who conquer foes, kill anyone in their way and serve up vengeance with delight in sequel after sequel. Meanwhile, we overlook the ways in which we see women nullified and brutalized around the world. For centuries victors of war have considered rape their right and privilege. An estimated 2,000,000 German women were raped by the invading Russians and American forces in 1945 and another 20,000 Chinese women were raped by invading forces in Nanking in 1937[8]. In the United States someone is sexually assaulted every 107 seconds. In a 2013, US News and World Report cited a United Nations-

---

[8] According to the Women's Media Center 2018.

funded survey[9] explaining the reasons for rape included sexual entitlement, a need for entertainment or to punish the subject. Participation in gangs and the need to express masculine dominance over women were also reported as factors in causing rape. Rape goes on today in peace time and at war despite public efforts to eliminate it. As long we foster the imbalance between the masculine and feminine this abuse is likely to continue.

It is staggering the degree to which we accept the primacy of the masculine and the diminution of the feminine in our world culture. Perhaps the most extreme cases are found in places like Saudi Arabia and parts of Asia but around the world it is an accepted fact that we will do things in a masculine way. Many of the ills of our society arise from this imbalance. I believe many corporations don't run well because they are too masculine. There's an old adage that when you only have a hammer every problem is a nail. This is where humanity finds itself today, solving every problem with action or aggression instead of trying more feminine approaches like allowing space and stillness.

---

[9] Jewkes, Rachel, et al. "Prevalence of and Factors Associated with Non-Partner Rape Perpetration: Findings from the UN Multi-Country Cross-Sectional Study on Men and Violence in Asia and the Pacific." *The Lancet Global Health*, vol. 1, no. 4, 2013, doi:10.1016/s2214-109x (13)70069-x.

This imbalance is responsible for a generalized sense of shame that all women feel. Even if our personal experiences haven't activated shame we are excusing ourselves simply for being women. Western women grew up with the story of Eve eating the apple and causing humanity's exile from Eden, her weakness is responsible for all the sufferings of humanity. Think about how powerfully this story colors the way we think of ourselves. Every day, every single item in the news could be viewed as the fault of women, little wonder we see ourselves as inherently flawed. This is why we endure domestic violence, don't speak up when think something is wrong, or agree to wrong-headed legislation that blames the victim for a rape. Today there is a virtual pandemic of harassment, sexual abuse and rape with no clear policies or societal will to change[10]. It is possible to restore society to health by viewing ourselves as out of balance, not as men and women but as people who are ignoring the full range of our humanity.

I was raised, as many girls were, on the mythology of the princess[11]. I watched Cinderella,

---

[10] I have intentionally omitted a discussion of sexual violence and shame. This topic has been covered in great detail by both survivors and scholars. This omission in no way suggests that this isn't an important topic. Find resources on sexual trauma in the back of this book.

[11] For more on this see *Cinderella Ate My Daughter: Dispatches from the Front Lines of the New Girlie-Girl Culture* by Peggy Orenstein

Snow White, and The Wizard of Oz and loved them all. As an adult when I examine these storylines I'm disturbed by the way I engaged in kind of societal brainwashing. The angry/dangerous/bitter witch/queen wants to destroy the beautiful/confident/smart princess (notice she is always the as yet uncrowned, i.e. a powerless, princess) who is eventually saved by the strong/charming/ powerful man and she lives happily ever after. There's a few things about these myths that contribute to our feelings of shame as women. First that older, strong woman is dangerous. Second, that youth and beauty are the most valuable things about a woman. Third that the princess isn't able to save herself and finally that when she is saved, her reason for being thereafter is to be a wife.

Don't get me wrong, I loved these stories, but as myths they significantly harmed my psyche. I grew up almost subconsciously thinking that to grow older, wiser and stronger was evil. I spent the better part of my teens and twenties in search of the man to complete me. I also genuinely believed that men, by virtue of being stronger, were better than me. Once I got married I was completely unprepared for the fact that marriage is difficult and my husband wasn't responsible for fixing me. These myths, along with the deluge of romantic comedies, leave no room for women to feel whole on their own or to have an unconventional relationship. Most of us go through life feeling that if we don't find a life partner we are incomplete. Hollywood has made some attempts at changing these perceptions but the most recent spate of movies about powerful women all included these old tropes about the importance of beauty and the need for a man in order to succeed on a mission. These movies are routinely lambasted, mostly by men, for being unrealistic or boring. Society's ability to visualize a woman as a power in her right is still profoundly limited.

If you look around you can see the damage these myths have done everywhere. Women desperately having plastic surgery to stave off the appearance of age. At least three former contestants from the very popular show The Bachelorette have committed suicide, when the dream of "happily ever after" didn't work out as planned. The average length of marriage[12] in the U.S. is eight years with 50% of marriages ending in divorce. I suspect the ideal of feminine powerlessness and innate rightness of the prince also contributes to women's tolerance of harassment and abuse.

Beginning in the 1960's the role of women began to change in Western countries. Women entered the work place, and politics and could be seen as leaving the home for a more expansive life. The

---

[12] I'm not endorsing marriage I'm only pointing out that once couples decide to marry something in our society is causing them to divorce.

challenge since then has been that while we have gained some equality outside the home the numerous responsibilities of maintaining a home still exist. It has been common to say that women want to do it all. I believe it is more accurate to say that women *feel they have to do it all.* I've always remembered a friend who had a successful career, two beautiful children and a happy marriage saying that she hadn't done anything *well* in years. She said, "I'm not very good at my job anymore, my kids hate me for going to work, my house is a disaster and we haven't had sex in months." It's terribly sad to think that this woman who was living the supposed American dream felt like a failure. This is the soul-killing situation many women find themselves in today.

Our feelings of not being enough in society begins long before work or parenthood. As a child growing up in Southern California I was acutely aware of the high standard of beauty I was supposed to represent. The expectation that you be thin, blond, tan and look great in a bikini was omnipresent for me. As a teenager, I worried incessantly about growing old and ordinary. By 16 or 17 I had a sense that time was slipping away from me, that my years being young and beautiful were the only good years in my life.

I grew up around the movie industry and at early age I knew that a woman's career in Hollywood ended at 30. Hollywood consistently casts women who are too young to realistically play men's wives and girlfriends. As a 30-year-old Catherine-Zeta-Jones played Sean Connery's love interest when he was 69. Between the years 1996 and 2006 Harrison Ford's leading ladies ranged between 14 and 27 years younger than him. This older man/younger woman dynamic sends a message that women aren't worthy love after a certain age. In magazines, in our entertainment and on the internet, we are bombarded with messages that older women are unworthy of attention and that their sexuality is repellent. When I say older I mean over 35 not 75. Women like Sophia Loren, Catherine Deneuve or Lauren Hutton who are still viewed as beautiful and sexy after 60 are often presented by the media as anomalies. This is hardly a comfort to the average women who never looked like a famous model to begin with. Most women approach middle age with a sense of resignation and grief. Many feel marginalized or simply invisible to society at large.

A further complication for women and their self-image is the excessive attention to our bodies. We endure a tidal wave of images of flat stomachs, perky bottoms and spectacular cleavage every day. Women see flawless perfection no matter where they turn, in every form the media. Many of us grow up associating happiness with a beautiful, thin body. It is socially acceptable to make fun of fat women both publically and privately. Women who are a normal weight or a few pounds overweight feel a profound sense of shame and failure. As one who suffered from eating disorders I always believed that a particular, magic number on the scale would equal a happy life.

I remember reading about the messy and painful divorce of a supermodel from her extremely rich husband. I remember being surprised that she was struggling despite her thinness and beauty. It sounds ridiculous when I see it written down but it shows how deeply ingrained my belief system is. On some cellular level, I genuinely believe that youth and beauty are the only path to happiness. The irony is that both are ephemeral, hardly a good place to store my self-esteem.

Women find themselves trying to solve an impossible puzzle to consider themselves valuable. They must be thin, beautiful, a good wife and mother, a stellar bread-winner, and remain young in the midst of it. It is impossible. I don't blame the media; I blame our culture which generates this image of women instead of valuing authenticity. I also blame us all for continuing to lap up entertainment that supports a one-dimensional view of women as subordinates either as a devoted underling, a victim, a damsel in distress, a vixen. or if she dares to speak up, a ball-buster.

Another strange conundrum of our femininity surrounds childbearing. For me it began with a secretive film in gym class when I was 12. I don't remember what the movie said but I do remember feeling ashamed of my period before it even started. Most women go around feeling they must keep menstruation a secret. For centuries women have been confined (even the word is telling) during their period and during pregnancy, exiled from society in way that seems unnatural. When you think of what we are actually doing, *continuing the species*, we should be, honored, cherished and celebrated. Somehow society has managed to pathologize reproduction, an entirely natural human function. Women are chastised and shamed for breast-feeding in public. Instead of celebrating our daughters' entrance into adulthood and the ability to reproduce we find ourselves delivering an illicit message of shame. Instead of celebrating mothers' courage and power we treat them as if they are weak and helpless. All of this leads to a profound sense of shame about having a female body.

As women, we must ask ourselves why this is okay with us? Why should the ability to bear and rear children be hidden from public view? Why do we permit violence against women to be entertainment? Why do we continue to watch the myth of the helpless princess in need of man? Why do we buy magazine with unnaturally thin women on the cover? Why do we participate when the press gets into a frenzy about how much weight a woman has gained or lost? Why do we buy products sold using misogynist ad campaigns? Why do we perpetuate a system that is clearly making us unhappy?

I honestly don't know the answer. I watch Law & Order re-runs which frequently feature violent crimes against women. I've bought clothes, make-up and accessories from companies that have aired offensive (or just plain dumb) advertising. I've looked at the pictures of Kim Kardasian gaining weight in pregnancy and Kate Bosworth plummeting below 100 pounds. I can't explain it, but I know that it isn't helping me and it isn't helping create a healthy society for women and the daughters we are raising.

It is possible to change the way we treat one another. Many of us have habits that have not contributed to our own sense of well-being. As women, we can support one another and support feminine principles[13]. We can encourage femininity when we see it expressed. Offer creating space, waiting or listening as an option instead of automatically leaping to *doing* something. Provide support for your son, brother or husband to be more feminine without criticism and try not to make them *do* something. Find ways to make it safe for people to be open around you without judgment or trying to fix their problem. Perhaps the most feminine quality

---

[13] For more on this topic you can purchase my book *The Wisdom of the Kitchen Manifesto.*

of all is just being open and nurturing without an agenda, simply allowing things to happen.

As a simple first step, we can refrain from commenting on the weight of celebrities or using unkind words about other women. We really aren't qualified to comment on another woman's life because we never really know what she's been through. We can avoid participating in conversations where women gossip about each other. We can stop giving insincere compliments and the backhanded insults. We can look around in our workplace or our neighborhood and see if there are women who could use encouragement and support. We can stop the familiar female habit of being exclusive and petty. We can offer our experience to other women in areas we have succeeded in. I long for women to find a way to help one another up instead of bullying and competing with one another. My years in corporate America included a series of disappointing betrayals by women I loved and considered friends. We are only hurting ourselves. We are only contributing to one another's shame. We can stop whenever we decide to.

And I Didn't Even Know I Was Freezing to Death

I've described the development of my sense of shame to help you recognize it in your own experience. From early in my childhood until middle age this was my personal operating system. I felt shame almost constantly. I was driven by perfectionism and the petty tyrant *Should*. I genuinely believed I was a mistake. I had spent almost 30 years struggling with anorexia, bulimia and overeating. I had grown very tired of being alive and though I was not suicidal I certainly wasn't enthusiastic about life.

Outwardly, my life was going fine. My career was successful. I had plenty of friends and a happy marriage. I had most of the elements of the American dream but I felt empty and unhappy. I knew that I wanted things to change.

At the time, I worked with a woman named Jan from another department. We worked together on the phone and decided it was time to meet face-to-face. One day she appeared in my doorway. She was a pretty blond, about 5'-10", who I guessed was about 50. She had something inexpressible that I found attractive. As I got to know her I noticed she was at ease with herself, always comfortable in her own skin. One of my co-workers told me that Jan had lost a lot of weight some years earlier. This, of course, increased my interest in discovering her secret. I screwed up my courage and I asked her how she had lost the weight, kept it off and why she was so happy. She told me honestly what she had done and she also told me it had taken many years for her to change. The punch line was that she was genuinely happy and enjoyed her life. Like an Eskimo who found me wandering the ice floes of the North Pole nearly frozen to death Jan brought me into her proverbial igloo and taught me how to survive.

I knew I was at the end of my rope. I had tried every kind of diet and exercise program. I had read a battery of self-help books, tried several different religious traditions and joined all kinds of social and professional organizations. Nothing made me feel good about myself. I decided to try Jan's approach for living. I finally faced the fact that I had eating disorders. I joined a support group, found a therapist, read many books and consulted with Jan and other people who seemed to have freedom from the shame and hopelessness that plagued me.

Almost my first order of business was to stop eating sugar which I recognized as my personal form of alcoholism. I couldn't eat just one piece of candy or brownie or cookie and I knew I ate sugar to help curb my emotions. Jan had helped me to see that my eating habits were clouding my judgment and preventing me from feeling my real feelings. I had an experience that was similar, though not as severe, to an addict withdrawing from alcohol or drugs. When I stopped eating sugar I was irritable, tired and headachy for about 3 weeks, but as my head cleared I began to see my life as it actually was. I also, to my dismay, began to feel things more keenly.

Very early in my recovery I realized that I was spiritually bankrupt. Although I had followed some religious traditions I didn't have a vibrant spiritual life. I tended to do things based on my own self will and I seldom asked for help or advice. I gradually surrendered to the realization I created most of the chaos and drama that I experienced in my own life. Eventually I found a spiritual path that made the rest of my recovery possible. Without it I doubt I would have made any lasting change.

Over the next several years, I began to see and do things differently. I collected a number of tools that helped me recover from the crippling shame I felt. The chapters that follow will help illuminate some of the most helpful ways I found to recover.

Part Two

Simple Tools to Help Deal with the Complicated Mess Known as Life

Neither More Than
Nor Less Than

I used to hate the word humility. I confused it with humiliation. I thought that to have humility meant to place myself beneath, or at the disposal of others. From my religious experience, I believed that humility was a desirable character trait, but I had never been able to make myself feel like I was less important than others. Somehow self-interest always seemed to overwhelm my best intentions.

One day I read this sentence in a daily devotional reader loaned to me by a friend

"It is easy to confuse certain desirable attributes with undesirable ones. To have humility, for example, does not mean to feel inferior. On the contrary, it means feeling equal – neither less nor more worthy than anyone[14]."

This quote presented what I considered to a revolutionary principle; equality. What if I truly was no better or no worse than anyone else? I

---

14 Source: For Today Overeaters Anonymous, Inc © 1982

thought about this for weeks and I began to see the ways that I was in a constant state of comparison with others. I realized that if I saw Charlize Theron on TV, I thought, "Oh I'm not as pretty as her." And if I saw a homeless man in front of Starbucks I thought, "Oh at least I'm not as bad off as him." Then one day it hit me: This is a game that will never end. There will always be someone better and someone worse. As long as I continued comparing myself I would always find myself, or someone else, lacking. What was worse, it meant that everywhere I went I was focused on myself, how I looked, how well off I was or if I was deprived of something.

I decided to try a new way of thinking. I had learned a few skills for re-programming my behavior and I watched my thoughts carefully for this kind of comparison thinking. Whenever I caught myself I would say, "neither more than nor less than." By doing this I recognized the near epidemic of comparison thinking in my life.

As I began to recover, I was working with high-level executives at my company. I noticed how I would walk in the room and start thinking how they made more money, knew more and were smarter than me. I tried to remember that I was neither more than nor less than anyone else in the room. My posture improved. My ability to speak up when I had a differing point-of-view increased. Most remarkable was that I was treated with more respect. Again and again executives who had previously treated me with indifference would turn to me for my opinion. Thinking of myself as an equal transformed the way others perceived me.

If you look up humility in the dictionary, you'll find that pride is a common antonym. This was the surprising outcome of recognizing true humility. I learned that I fueled my pride by thinking about myself in comparison to others all the time. As I gradually learned to give up comparison thinking I thought about myself less. I became less defensive and felt less need to assert my will on others. Being an equal was a huge relief. It meant I didn't have something to prove anymore.

Also around this time I began meditating. I found that 5 minutes of sitting quietly was liberating. Gradually my thinking became less *sticky*. I found that I wouldn't get so lost in story lines about what others had or did not have. I was able to simply recognize that I was fabricating a story line and let it go. In order to help refrain from building up story lines, I realized I needed to stop reading certain magazines. I found that looking at the fabulous lives of some celebrities didn't help me. Every time I saw their beautiful children, the breathtaking view from their living room or their seemingly perfect marriage I felt like less than. So, I simply stopped buying magazines that fueled my feeling of being less than. Today, many years later I still skip certain magazines on the newsstand and I really don't miss the crushing feeling of being less than.

Seeing Eye to Eye

One of the symptoms of shame is an inability to meet the gaze of others. I found it very difficult to look people in the eye when I was suffering from shame. I would force myself to do it in settings like job interviews or negotiations but generally I avoided the direct or prolonged gaze of others. I would always look away because it felt unbearable to be seen.

At the crux of this discomfort is the concept that 'The eyes are the window of the soul[15]'. I had difficulty looking others in the eye because I didn't want them to see inside me. I felt that my life was too messy and that my essence was not likeable. I knew that I was prone to anger, selfishness and impatience. I was desperate to hide this from those close to me. I wanted everyone to see me as a nice, helpful, good natured, patient girl. I feared if they looked me in the eye they would see that that this wasn't true.

Around this time, I started working with a meditation instructor who taught me how to hold the gaze of another person. We would be sitting quietly or talking and he would look me directly in the eye and hold my gaze. Initially, I found it unbearable and I would look away in a few

---

[15] Matthew 6:22-23

seconds. My heart would beat faster and I would feel like running away. He persisted and over time I found that I was able to look back at him. I tried looking others in the eye for short periods of time and I found, to my surprise, that most people are friendly. Allowing them to look at me, in the eye, was actually pleasant. I don't do this perfectly but now I know that when I'm afraid to look someone in the eye that I am experiencing shame. If I'm unable to look someone in the perhaps I have said or done something harmful. In other cases, it's that old habit of comparison, I might believe that someone is prettier, smarter, thinner or more accomplished. I still suffer from the fear of being seen for who I really I am. The process is less than perfect but I always try to recognize the progress.

Meet the Self Sisters

"Humility is not thinking less of yourself, it's thinking of yourself less." This quote is often attributed to C.S. Lewis and it matches my personal experience. I have found relief from my longtime companions, the Self Sisters; Self-Pity, Selfishness, Self-Centeredness, Self-Righteousness and Self Will. These five had been wreaking havoc in my life for years and I often acquiesced to their demands. I never really liked them and yet I continued to offer them a guest room in my mind.

Self-Pity

The martyr story line is sustained by self-pity. For me, this was always the first sister I would go to. Even as a young child I would resort to feeling sorry for myself at the slightest provocation. If my mother asked me to clean my room I felt it was unfair, that other kids didn't have to clean their room, that I was somehow being singled out. When I think about this behavior, I always picture myself hunkering down in a hole and licking my wounds. It keeps up an almost constant banter about how I am misunderstood, unloved, or unable to do what others do. Self-pity helped me be in constant state of blaming others. My "poor me" story shifted the responsibility from me to others. Whatever situation I found myself in it was because someone else put me there. The sad outcome of this kind of thinking is a sense of general powerlessness. *I am always a victim. I can't affect the outcome of the situations in my life. I can't help what other people say and do.* The irony of this kind of thinking is that it is exactly backwards. In fact, we can change every situation in the way that we think about it.

Dictionary definitions of self-pity include the concept that self-pity is a state of being excessively absorbed by one's own troubles. The underlying idea is that we should not have to experience the pain and discomfort that is an ordinary part of life. In some cases we may feel that we lack the confidence or competence to deal with these situations. It is normal to experience some self-pity, what isn't healthy is to stay in it. It is important to adopt strategies that will help you move in to acceptance of whatever it is that is causing you to feel sorry for yourself.

Many years ago, I had the occasion to meet a minister who had been held hostage in the Middle East. He spent 16 months in captivity chained to a radiator with a sack over his head. His presence was extraordinarily powerful. It was clear to me that he had emerged from the experience as a victor not a victim. When I asked him how he survived he said that he had spent almost every day praying. He would use the links of the chain like a rosary advancing up the links and praying for individuals, institutions and nations every day. Although he was mistreated he never felt like a victim and he viewed his captivity as a way to enhance his spiritual life. Looking in his eyes it was possible to see the light of a genuine spiritual enlightenment. I was always struck by his complete lack of resentment toward his captors, in fact he felt compassion for the pain that had driven them to such an unreasonable act. He could have retreated into self-pity but instead he chose a path in which he was still the master of his own mind.

A simple exercise to help work through self-pity is to ask yourself the following questions:

1. *What is bothering me or making me unhappy?*

2. *Why is that circumstance making me unhappy?*

3. *What can I do change this? (If the answer is 'nothing' then your only choice is to move gracefully toward acceptance.)*

4. *When you complete these questions take the steps necessary to improve the situation as soon as reasonably possible.*

Self-Centeredness

The myth of Narcissus is the tragic story that illustrates the perils of falling in love with one self. Being self-centered is the inability to adopt the viewpoint of others and being self-centered is exaggerating my own importance. Narcissism is an extreme case of self-centeredness which is actually classified as a mental disorder. This can lead to strong reactions to criticism or requiring constant approval or attention. People who are self-centered often take advantage of others to achieve their own ends. I see it as being distinct from selfishness because it always places Me at the center of the story. Self-centeredness is about my perspective, while selfishness is about my actions. I thought the movie, *Bridesmaids* was hilarious although it was a portrait of a hero who was entirely self-centered. Although it was not Kristin Wiig's wedding, she made herself the center of the story and a good deal of suffering ensued.

In order to help diffuse my natural self-centeredness I have begun trying to see things from the perspective of others. I ask myself what someone else may want or need. I try not to see myself as the center of every story. This means I don't interject comments into conversation as frequently as I used to. One of my mantras now is, "It's not about me." It is amazing the degree of relief I get from this simple statement. The snippy teller at the bank, my husband's anger at the broken printer, my boss's reaction to a meeting that goes poorly, when I recognize it is not about me I find relief. If it's something I've done, I have a chance to get a clearer perspective to see how my actions affect others.

Selfishness

The quality of selfishness is placing my interests above everyone else's. Where self-centered is the way we think, selfishness is the way we act. It is being devoted to my own agenda and acting accordingly. It is natural, even healthy, for us to watch out for our own well-being. Aside from our parents no one else is responsible for making sure we are okay. But, selfishness carries this to an extreme. We become so concerned about our own well-being that we disregard the needs of others. In a civil society that is not a welcome characteristic, from time to time we need to surrender to the needs of others. As long as we are trapped in a self-centered viewpoint it is difficult for us to experience any compassion or empathy.

One of the ways I have found to diffuse selfishness is to intentionally surrender to the needs of others. When I catch that strong feeling that I want some specific thing, I try leaving it for someone else. Because of my years of eating disorders, I always assess which cut of meat I want or which piece of bread looks best. It has become a great exercise to allow myself to be served and not to take what I want. What I try to do is avoid situations where I am manipulating things to my own ends. If I really want to go to the Sandra Bullock movie and my husband really wants to see James Bond I try to yield. It's important for my well-being not to always get my way.

One caution is that I don't do this all the time. IF I have a healthy self-image, I should know what I want and how to get it. After a good deal of therapy and talking to friends who have good self-esteem I have become better and better at distinguishing between healthy self-care and selfishness. It takes practice and I recommend using small things with low stakes. The best way to start is with small acts like putting others first, allow someone to go ahead of you in a line at the store or do a chore that your spouse or roommate normally does. Gradually, these small acts will add up to real change in your behavior.

Self-Righteousness

Self-righteousness springs from a strong belief in being right or morally superior. It is often apparent in political and religious situations but it is far more pervasive than that. Anytime we express certainty that our position is right we are in danger of being self-righteous. It can be seen in situations where we don't like a friend's new boyfriend or the color they painted their house. Self-righteousness is often evident in situations where we think others should or shouldn't be doing something. It is often associated with situations where people believe in a set of governing rules that they either agree or disagree with. Behold the strong emotions that flow freely at a home owner's association meeting or a school planning meeting and you're likely to be encountering self-righteousness.

Society is based on all of us observing and obeying certain norms, like driving on the correct side of the road, but self-righteousness carries this too far. Self-righteousness often involves blame. Others are not doing what they could and should be doing and you believe, something will go wrong as a result. Judging, tattling, and gossiping are common behaviors associated with self-righteousness. Often we engage in these behaviors because of low self-esteem. We don't believe that we are okay or will be okay in the future. Focusing our attention on others deflects our discomfort.

For me self-righteousness often arises in situations where I am afraid or uncertain. I find myself shouting at the television when I don't like what I hear on the news. Most of the things I yell about are things that make me feel powerless because I don't know the solution. It's important for me to slow down and acknowledge I'm afraid before I start offering opinions about who should be doing what.

Self-righteousness has a dangerous ally in anger. Many times when I encounter something I don't like I get mad. When I drive anywhere outside of Los Angeles I find myself getting annoyed at other drivers on the road. I groan at their inability to merge or that they are driving 50 mph in the left lane. I can feel my boiling sense of superiority because *people don't know how to drive.* In truth, what I mean is people in other cities *don't drive like me.* I have adopted a strong belief in my moral superiority because of how I drive. The irony is that my resentment towards other drivers is only hurting me. Resentment is like taking poison and hoping the other person will die.

The best way to begin to diffuse self-righteousness is to examine moments where you are angry or judgmental. Whenever I'm angry I try to pause and notice if something frightened me. Nine times out of ten this is the cause of my anger. When I feel I don't have any control I'm often afraid. Recognizing and accepting this as a fact of life has helped me learn to manage my fear.

It is also helpful to notice when you believe you know better than someone else. We often judge ourselves more leniently because we understand our own thoughts and motives. When we look at someone else we aren't able to know for certain what they think or why they are doing what they are doing. The most important way to give up self-righteous behavior is to begin to see yourself with kindness and compassion. My experience is that my tolerance for others' weaknesses is directly proportionate to my tolerance for myself and my weaknesses. Meditation has been the best tool I've found to improve my self-esteem.

Self-Will

Self-will involves molding the environment to suit my own needs. It starts with a mindset that says "I know best." It can be as simple as deciding which route I think should be used to drive to an event or as complicated as manipulating co-workers in order to get a promotion. Self-will is like an unhappy toddler that will scream until it gets what it wants. Self-will precludes the possibility that there is a higher power, a boss, a parent, a spouse or a God. The way things should go begins and ends with Me. Like selfishness it precludes having empathy or compassion for others but it also expresses an excess of pride. It is the inability to be flexible, accept other viewpoints or appreciate the thoughts and feelings of others. I tended to operate in the self-will mode most of the time. I've always been a natural leader and people look to me to take charge which I considered a license rather than a gift. This kind of thinking precluded me from seeing alternative approaches and kept me from relaxing and enjoying life's mysteries. I've learned that often things even better than I imagined arise if I just allow them to unfold. All the situations that I felt I needed to take charge of turned out just fine without any intervention from me.

My husband has a quote posted on the refrigerator that says "If you don't want what you have, don't do what you did." This is the trap of self-will. As long as I continue to operate in self-will I will keep getting the same unsatisfactory results.

The best way of minimizing self-will has been to ask for advice and then *take it*. Inside of me there is a strong willed three-year-old who always says "I do it" or "I know." No matter what the circumstance she always steps up, I finally realized that an adult needed to take charge. An adult knows that there are alternative perspectives. An adult asks for help from others who have experience with the situation. There have been times, many of them, when I've received advice from a friend, a supervisor or a spiritual teacher and my first thought is always, "You don't know as much about the situation as I do." Of course, this is true, but disregarding advice and wisdom is still not a healthy practice. My therapist suggested to try some of her suggestions before I decided that I knew better. I was shocked at how effective her ideas were. Over time I gained the courage to try doing things that others suggested, particularly when they had success in areas where I had failed. I realized by surrendering self-will things often turned out better.

Self-will also precludes the possibility of something greater than myself. As I've enhanced my spiritual life I've found that my reliance on a greater power has increased. Understanding God/Great Spirit/the Force/Supreme Being has more power than I do has also been an important transformation. Some of my self-will arose from a sense of hyper-responsibility. Believing in a power beyond myself has eased the feeling that I need to take care of everything. Believing you will be divinely take care of no matter what will diminish the power of self-will.

One of the benefits to reducing self-will has been that I no longer feel responsible for every situation. I often sit back and let others decide. To my surprise, I've discovered new experiences and new ways of doing things. I've learned in the most delightful way, that my way is not the best way, it is just one alternative. Giving up self-will, at least some of the time, has been a relief.

I've slowly begun to move towards genuine humility. I've learned the truth that I really am *neither more than nor less* than anyone else. For months, I marked a tiny equal symbol on the inside of my wrist with a permanent marker. When I noticed it during the day it was a reminder not to compare myself to others, to think I am superior to others, or to succumb to focusing solely on myself. These old habits were ingrained and I needed to train myself to think in a new way. Gradually I've learned a healthier way of thinking.

The Unsexy Ways You Talk Dirty to Yourself

There is no single habit that contributes more to the development of shame than negative self-talk. For years, I kept up a steady negative internal dialogue that poisoned everything I thought and most of my actions. The worst part is that it was like a cancer in my thinking. I wasn't even aware it was growing and flourishing inside of me. Many of these things are never said aloud which, in some ways, makes them even more deadly.

Most negative self-talk flows directly from habitual thinking that we aren't even aware of. One of the keys to recovering from shame is spotting this kind of thinking and finding techniques to diffuse it. Habitual thinking is tricky because it is your perception, and you have to catch your own perceptions to stop it. Like the protagonist in 'A Beautiful Mind' who couldn't fix the trouble with his brain because the trouble *was* his brain.

My therapist taught me to identify and name any kind of detrimental thinking and then say to myself, aloud if possible, "I'm not going to hurt myself by thinking this way." I call this the Universal Antidote to negative self-talk. Since learning this technique I have passed it on to many friends. We have all had similar experiences of improved self-image as a result of using this one simple sentence. This can be applied to all of the negative thinking patterns listed below.

There are three broad categories for these kinds of habitual thoughts that are like unwelcome internal radio stations who feed you unhelpful and inaccurate information almost every day.

The Deluded Despot

The Deluded Despot is a cruel, autocratic ruler who provides nothing but confused and arbitrary information. The Deluded Despot encourages you to believe in a world view that life is overly simple. It suggests that it is possible to a have final, predictable outcomes. The Deluded Despot's world is very small, and every road is narrow and one-way. The Deluded Despot generates absolutist thinking, using all-or-nothing language that includes words like 'always,' 'never,' 'win,' 'lose,' or 'fail'. Another good signal of this absolutist thinking is the use of the words like 'disaster' and 'perfect' to describe events and circumstances.

Nobody likes a tyrannical ruler, and the one telling you everything is finite is not your friend. Here are some examples of habitual thoughts that The Deluded Despot might feed you and some antidotes to overcome these and similar thoughts.

If I can't do it perfectly, I won't even try

You may see outcomes as absolute without gradation. If your performance falls short of perfect, you may consider yourself a failure. It often includes a competitive mindset that perceives life experiences as win or lose. This kind of thinking is characterized by contingencies and ultimatums. Your language may have 'or else' embedded in it, often taking yourself and others hostage with your ideas.

For me, this was reflected in my unwillingness to try anything unless I was sure I would succeed. Because of my inner perfectionist, I couldn't bear the idea of failing at something. For years, I made excuses about why I hadn't tried snow skiing or golf but the truth was that I knew these were difficult skills to acquire. When I look back, I feel a sense of regret about all the things I never tried because I was afraid I couldn't do them perfectly.

Antidotes

• *Try something new that's hard for you and learn it slowly.*
• *Notice when you make a mistake, and acknowledge that you are just learning, then keep going.*
• *Beware of turning things into a competition.*

There are only two possible outcomes — one is good, one is bad

You see all situations as binary or having only two possible outcomes. You seek to simplify situations which may be complex and have opposing, but equally valid sides. This is sometimes called the false dilemma and is characterized by statements like 'Either you are my friend or my enemy.' This is closely related to winner-take-all thinking except that it extends beyond the idea of success or failure to almost every outcome in life. This kind of thinking precludes the possibility of gray areas.

What if there is no right answer? What if there is an equally appealing third alternative? What if these are not two ideas in opposition to one another? What if this situation is too complex for a simple black-and-white answer? This kind of unconditional thinking was really unfamiliar to me. I was in a constant state of setting up opposing alternatives. The truth is that many of life's decisions are ambivalent, there may be two, or three, or five equally appealing options. One trick I learned from a friend is to ask "Is there a third choice?" To my surprise and delight; there often is.

Antidotes
- *Try to think of a third option.*
- *Accept the gray and the in-between.*

❧❧

I feel it, so it must be true

You make your emotions the truth and use circumstances to bolster your feelings. You believe you must act on something just because you have a feeling.

Like many people, when I stand on the top of a high building I recognize how easy it would be to jump off. The distorted way of thinking would be to jump just because I felt like I might jump. I have often felt a compulsive need to do things just because I thought of them. As an addict, when I think of the thing I crave I believe that it's too late, now that I've had the thought I have to use.

I often thought people were mad at me. If someone was rude or just didn't particularly notice me, I would assume I had done something wrong and spiral into a negative emotional tail spin. Then I would continue to interpret their actions through my own emotional state. The trouble was, because I *felt* something, I thought it was true. Because I believed my feelings were absolute facts and I fueled a cycle of listening to them and reacting to them, no matter how inaccurate they were. It took me years to recognize that my feelings were not facts.

When I began meditating, I felt I had clearer perceptions of what was happening: I discovered how often my storyline was inaccurate. My husband wasn't mad at me; he was just hungry. My friend hadn't stopped speaking to me; she was busy at work. The emotional charge of these inaccurate perceptions drained out when I started to see that just because I felt something, particularly a negative emotion, it didn't mean it was true.

Antidotes
• *A useful mantra is "Feelings are not facts."*

❧

I think I should, therefore I have to do it

You believe that you can motivate yourself by saying "should." You have the false belief that somewhere there is a scoreboard and you are required to do certain things to keep up. When you apply this thinking to other people it fosters expectations, resentments and anger. The unpleasant byproduct is guilt and shame.

I've given numerous examples of the *Tyranny of Should* earlier in the book and I've included it here as a part of the overview of The Deluded Despot. Whenever you hear any 'should' words coming up in your thoughts or language proceed with caution. I often say the best place for "should" is when following laws. You should pay your taxes. You ought to drive the speed limit. Otherwise, use another, *better* word.

If I find my schedule is packed full or that I'm dreading upcoming events, this is evidence of the presence of Should. Focusing on things I want to do and things that genuinely need to be done makes it easier to say "No" to things I feel obligated to. Sometimes I weigh alternatives against one another. *If I accept the responsibility to organize this fundraiser, will it cut into the time I have to work on my next book?* Saying No to some good things can be a healthy choice that preserves your ability to do other equally good things.

Antidotes
* *Try to eliminate 'Should,' 'Must,' 'Ought,' 'Always,' and 'Never' from your vocabulary.*
* *Try using 'May,' 'Might,' and 'Sometimes.'*
* *Learn to say "No."*

❧❦

There's only a finite amount of ____ in the world, and I probably won't get what I need

You believe that the universe is limited and that you need to rely only on yourself to make sure you are taken care of. You live with a sense of fear that you won't have enough. This can cause you to be competitive or to experience constant worry.

As long as I can remember, I have worried about not getting my share. As a child, I worried that I wouldn't get a piece of the cake at the party. As an adult, I was afraid there weren't enough men around for me to find a date or get married. Later I worried about my employer being unable to pay me or not getting a bonus. At the root of this fear of scarcity was an excessive sense of self-reliance. I genuinely believed that if I didn't take care of myself no one else would.

The Deluded Despot tells me that if others get something, like a promotion, then it won't happen for me. If I don't save my seat in the front row, if I don't buy this shirt I love, if I don't make plans for my birthday then someone else will get what I really want.

This also shows up as a discomfort with spending money. I wear clothes that have holes in them and hang on to things years after their usefulness because I'm afraid that I will need them later. Underneath this behavior is the belief that everything is about to run out and at some distant time in the future, I won't have any money to replace it.

I've gotten better but I still find myself fearing that I won't be cared for. I've even found that I am provided for situations that aren't necessarily monetary. One example happened when my mom had an accident while traveling in Ireland and I had only 18 hours to get to the hospital in Ireland before she went into surgery. On the morning of my departure a massive storm hit the East Coast and my flight was grounded. I asked a ticket agent if there was another way for me to get to Dublin. She looked at screen and said, "That's funny. There's a flight leaving for Chicago in an hour. It isn't a normally scheduled flight but last night it had to be held over so the crew could rest. I can put you on that one and you can catch a connection to Dublin from there." It turned out that only one flight went to Dublin from the U.S. that day, the one I got on.

I know the crew was grounded just so I could get on the flight, but I like the idea that by divine providence I was able to catch a flight when my mom really needed me. It's easy to discount this kind of miraculous intervention, except I've had this kind of thing happen hundreds of times. I've also had experienced where complete strangers helping me with simple things like handing me money I dropped on the ground and larger experiences like offering me a place to stay. The trick is to notice when it's happening.

Most of the time I do get what I'm hoping for so the idea that I won't isn't supported by fact. The Deluded Despot keeps me provoking a fear if I don't recognize it and manage my thoughts.

Antidotes

• *Cultivate gratitude.*
• *Use the mantra "I have enough, I do enough, I am enough."*

• *Use the Positive Evidence Locker[16].*

ন্ত্ৰ

The Unreliable Storyteller

The Unreliable Storyteller consistently misinterprets events and provides partial, inaccurate or just plain false information. Because we all love stories we are easily taken in by storytellers. Inside of our head we have a voice that is constantly generating stories, it's part of how we make sense out of our world. Many of us have great difficulty separating the false narrative from the facts. We continually alter our perception of actual events to maintain our shame storyline. If someone tells us we've made a mistake we immediately view all of life through that lens.

A great example of The Unreliable Storyteller can be seen on one of the procedural law T.V. shows when a lawyer examines a witness and twists the facts to suit their own narrative. The witness protests, "That's not what I meant! That's not what I said!"

The trouble for us is that we don't even protest, we just accept the false version we tell ourselves and carry on with our lives. Like the opposing

---

[16] For an explanation of the Positive Evidence Locker see the chapter *Taming that Bitch in Your Head*

counsel, cross-examining our thoughts, identifying false narratives as they arise, and refuting them is the key. Turning an inquisitive eye on own thinking will begin to diffuse its power.

Notice how the Unreliable Storyteller lurks at the fringes of your habitual thoughts whispering half-truths and unsubstantiated rumors. A great general approach to silence the Unreliable Storyteller is to ask yourself "Is that true?" and "What evidence do I have that it's true?" Gradually we will can craft a new storyline and approach the Unreliable Storyteller with healthy skepticism.

I'm such a loser/idiot/fraud or _____.

You curse yourself with belittling words and phrases, often things you would never say out loud to another human being. You call yourself negative and demeaning names like 'idiot' or characterize your own behavior in a negative light using critical words like 'lazy' or 'stupid.'

I call this Self-Slander because we say things about ourselves that simply aren't true. If put to any kind of rigorous test they would be found false. This is an example of adopting a false narrative by using a few instances to infer character flaws and permanent personal failings. This kind of thinking is often fueled by a false sense of humility. We think if we put ourselves down we won't get too egotistical. Notice that, in fact, these statements cause you to think more about yourself, not less. You may even try to fix your mistake or solve the perceived problem that doesn't actually exist.

We sometimes use this kind of negative thinking is to try to motivate ourselves. We think by running ourselves down, we will be motivated to do better. But ask yourself if that really works. If you were trying to teach someone a new skill would you heckle them when they made a mistake? If you were teaching a child, would you motivate them by saying, "You idiot" every time they tried? Now, ask yourself, why you think this name calling will motivate you.

For years, I engaged in almost constant self-slander and degrading self-talk. If I got lost I'd say, "You idiot, you always get lost." If I forgot to do something, I'd say, "I'm so stupid." This kind of thinking served to reinforce the idea that I am innately a mistake. Instead of saying, "Oops, I made a mistake," I would expand any mistake into a referendum of what was wrong with Stephanie. Gradually, I learned to stop using these unkind names and to even use language instead that acknowledges things I do well.

Cursing is defined as a solemn utterance intended to inflict harm. Talking to ourselves unkindly is actually cursing ourselves. The reverse would be to bless ourselves in difficult moments with words of encouragement, support and approval. This doesn't mean that we are bragging or inflating our sense of self; it means we choose to not inflict further harm on ourselves.

Once you notice this habit of self-slander, you'll hear it around you all the time. Women are particularly prone to say unkind about themselves. When you do observe unkind talk, pay attention to how it makes you feel to hear it. I find that I feel sad for the person who says these hurtful things about themselves. Life is hard enough without using self-abusive language.

Antidotes

• *Accept your mistakes as normal human behavior.*
• *Try motivating yourself with accurate positive statements about yourself and your behavior.*
• *Try blessing yourself instead of cursing yourself.*

ॐ

I'm not good at math/sports/_____

You extend a single event or situation, usually negative, to all the circumstances of your life. You pre-judge a situation based on non-specific, overly general information. This kind of thinking makes you prejudiced towards the circumstances of life.

Like many people, I found the concepts of algebra difficult to grasp. Every time my teacher said, "You are solving for x," I had no idea what he meant. No matter how hard I tried, algebra just didn't make sense to me. I lost interest in math and I never took advanced algebra or trigonometry. I began to say that I was not good at math.

Then in college, I got good grades in statistics and economics but I still thought I was bad at math. Now, as an adult, I have to solve algebra problems daily. I add and subtract fractions, and calculate how much gas is left in my car. All of these activities require math skills. It turns out that I'm actually good at math and algebra. I just didn't understand my algebra teacher. I pre-judged all math based on one bad experience. This is an example of excessive generalizing about myself

It also possible to generalize about other people or about situations. When I moved to Virginia, a clerical error at my insurance agent's office caused me to lose my car insurance, and I had pay a higher rate for my new insurance. For years, I hated that insurance company, and I would tell anyone who would listen not to use them, because they were terrible. The truth was that one person made a mistake, a mistake which I had the opportunity to catch and correct if I had read the paperwork more carefully. Because

I overgeneralized and interpreted this one negative event as a pattern, I spent years hating and bad-mouthing this company. I'm sure this reflected more poorly on me than it did on them.

Antidotes

Notice biases you have about a situation, an organization or person.

Be inquisitive and ask if yourself if you are applying past experience to the current situation too broadly.

Start fresh in the present moment.

છ્જ

Things are probably going to turn out badly

You enter situations with a false narrative, filter out or discount positive information and exaggerate negative information to support your negative theory.

Most people know the donkey, Eeyore, from The Winnie the Pooh[17] stories. His view is always colored by misfortune as he greets visitors with a perpetual negative filter. "Good morning" he says, "If it is a good morning, which I doubt."

This is the perspective of the permanent negative narrative. It is pretty easy to pick out what is

---

[17] *Winnie the Pooh,* by A.A. Milne ©1926

wrong with any situations. We are physiologically wired to scan our environment for potential threat. This was a useful skill when we could be killed by a predator but in modern society where many risks are less deadly, our minds are often assessing problems incorrectly.

When I worked as a business consultant, I prided myself on my ability to identify organizational problems. One day a mentor said, "Stephanie, most people are good identifying problems. The challenge is figuring out the solution."

This is the shift that's required to deal with this thinking. Realize that you *can* identify problems but that it doesn't serve you to continue *focusing* only on the problems. It's always possible to construct a negative storyline, but is it true? This mental habit takes an event like 'I wasn't picked for the kickball team' and turns it into 'I'm always the last one to be picked.' Take a moment and notice this kind of thinking. It is usually informed by a single event, not by the pattern you perceive.

It's also important to recognize your character traits are part of a continuum. If some people describe you as bossy, others may see you as a leader. Being described as a shy introvert could also mean you are discerning and thoughtful. Part of the issue many of us have is judging ourselves very harshly, and then extending that to a universal truth about who we are. Releasing your negative story lines can be very liberating.

Antidotes
- *Notice the tendency to turn an ordinary non-event into something with more dramatic meaning.*
- *Ask yourself, "How many times has this actually happened?"*
- *Balance the negative ideas with facts.*

❧❧

Thanks for the compliment but you don't really know me

You are likely to discount positive feedback and experiences and focus instead on the negative. This kind of thinking disregards and distorts facts, particularly positive ones.

Whenever my grandmother received a compliment on her appearance, she would invariably announce what a great deal she got on her dress. This is another expression of false humility. This is not just an inability to accept a compliment, it involves discounting positive feedback. We often discount compliments because we feel uncomfortable and want to deflect attention. It's a narrative that diminishes who we are.

One day, I was talking to a woman I hadn't met

before. As we chatted, she complimented me on my listening skills. I immediately began to explain how I wasn't really a good listener and that I was self-absorbed. Another friend turned to me and said "The only appropriate response to a compliment is, 'Thank you'." This is one of the hundreds of ways that I minimized the positive to keep the storyline going that I am deeply flawed. Learning to let compliments in is a discipline that has helped me to combat this kind of extreme thinking.

Antidotes

• *Say 'thank you' and nothing more when you receive a compliment.*
• *Examine the positive evidence.*
• *Check out your thinking with others.*

❧☙

I have a name for this person, situation or behavior

You give a person, situation or circumstance a label that may be inaccurate or excessive, and then cast it in concrete. You use overly strong language to describe something, often incorrectly.

As pattern-seeking animals, we try to order the information we receive into some coherent pattern. The ability to discern differences is a natural part of the development of the human brain. Categorizing is a natural part of being a human reasoning which isn't a problem until we carry it too far.

The most troublesome form of false labeling is identifying a person (including yourself), situation or behavior in a negative light, and then solidifying that idea. Once you use labels such as *lazy, insensitive* or *indecisive,* you leave them in that category. This precludes the possibility of that person being or doing something different. Oskar Schindler, of *Schindler's List,* was arguably greedy, self-interested and arrogant but his story points out he was also compassionate, loyal and fiercely protective. The story invites us to look at a multifaceted character and examine our own labels.

In our daily lives, we are inclined to categorize to make ourselves more comfortable. Once we have labeled (or in many cases mislabeled) something, we feel less ambivalence and anxiety. However, this fix is only temporary because people and situations are in a state of constant flux. It may be true that someone failed to keep a commitment. It doesn't mean that they always fail to keep commitments or, in the case of mislabeling, that they hate you and are out to get you. Each situation is influenced by millions of independent circumstances and is unlikely to happen again.

A helpful way to cope with this thinking is to watch your mind as it invents a story or a pattern. Acknowledge the injustice, pain or frustration of the current situation, allow yourself to feel the discomfort, anxiety or anger, and then move on to the next situation.

You can also examine the accuracy of your labels. I find that my most emotionally charged labels are often related to another person or an earlier situation, not the situation at hand. When I say someone is 'manipulative' what I really mean is, 'I haven't acknowledged times in the past I felt manipulated, and now I'm really angry it is happening again.' I can solve this problem by simply adding the word "sometimes" or "sometimes I feel" to my description.

Another reason we use labels is to cover our discomfort with my own behavior. One of my friends taught me a helpful phrase, "You spot it, you got it," meaning what we accuse others of is often what we do ourselves. The result is that I feel more comfortable with my own behavior, but only temporarily. It is far healthier for me to recognize my own failings and recognize the pain of our common human foibles.

Antidotes
• *Use the mantra, "This, too, shall pass" or "Feelings are not facts."*
• *Try modifying your descriptions with*

"sometimes" and "lately."

⁊◦⊱

This situation is actually about me, caused by me or they must be thinking and talking about me

You take things personally. You see yourself as the cause of some problem, or take on someone's opinion as having more value than it does.

I once did a large project for a client, during the course of launching their business, they ran out of money and decided not to pay me. For years, I berated myself for being a bad business owner, for not doing the work perfectly, and for not collecting the bad debt. I often said it was the worst thing that ever happened to me professionally. I magnified a single non-paying client into a major negative narrative. When I allowed myself to see that they simply ran out of money, and that it wasn't about me, I felt free.

Making it personal is commonplace. In traffic, we might assume that someone cuts us off because we are driving too slow or is being aggressive towards us. At work, we think that our boss doesn't like us, and that's why we are given an unpleasant project.

With this kind of thinking, we attach an inappropriate amount of importance to our own role in circumstances. We begin with the assumption we have done something wrong, or someone is out to get us, and we are suffering the consequence of our inherent failure. We see things through a lens which continually casts us as a failure, a victim or a villain.

Antidotes

•*Use the mantra "It's not about me" or the acronym Q-TIP for "Quit Taking It Personally"*
•*Review the objective facts of the situation*
•*Practice standing up straight, particularly when expressing an opinion or encountering negative opinions.*

🙥🙢

This is the worst thing that ever happened to me. I screwed up the most important moment of my life

You exaggerate small mistakes or magnify the attention on an individual event or events in your life. You turn ordinary events and mistakes into catastrophes. You exaggerate the failure or harm done.

When it comes to our thoughts, size matters. We make things bigger than they are. We make ourselves smaller than we are. We make things into disasters when they aren't. These kinds of thinking are inaccurate perceptions of reality. This thinking often uses words like "disaster", "catastrophe" and modifiers like "huge", "gigantic" and "epic".

If I have a headache, I assume it's a brain tumor. If I have a bad job interview, I've ruined my career. Notice how this thinking aligns with creating a story line that involves drama. If I oversleep my day is ruined[18].

I was working for a company that received some very negative news. As I watched the stock drop and read newspaper accounts of the potential lay-offs, I began to picture myself as a bag lady living under a bridge. I talked to a friend about my worries and she said, "Do you think you could get on the local train instead of immediately jumping on the express train to the end of the line?" This is catastrophic thinking leaps from right now to the worst possible conclusion.

Many years ago, my husband and I went through a very difficult financial time. We had to allow our health insurance to lapse, we paid our rent

---

[18] I have a friend who combats this by saying, "I never say I'm having a bad *day*, I'm not willing to surrender a whole day to one bad moment."

late and we dug quarters out of the sofa to buy groceries. When things got better, I told the story about the terrible time we had gone through. One day, as I was repeating this story, I stopped mid-sentence when I realized that I viewed it completely backwards. I had always told this story as the time of disaster. I said how I felt abandoned by God and completely alone.

Now, I realized that wasn't true at all. We had never missed a car or a rent payment, and although our health insurance lapsed we never needed it. We never even missed a meal. Far from being helpless and destitute, we had survived. The same facts could be looked at from a different perspective. I could see the positive outcome for the first time.

One way to combat this damaging thinking is to recall similar situations from the past. Have I been taken care of in the past? Have I achieved something despite the fact I thought I would fail? Have I recovered from illness and injury? This is all positive evidence that can contribute to my knowledge that something positive is likely to happen again.

Antidote

- *Use the mantra "Nothing bad is happening right now" or ask yourself "This is right, why is it right?"*
- *Cultivate gratitude. Try making a gratitude list.*
- *Examine the positive evidence.*

•Stay in the present moment, don't borrow trouble from the future.

ὡᘇᔦ

The Pseudo Superhero

The Pseudo Superhero tells we are capable of superhuman feats like predicting the future, mind-reading and fixing others' problems. Perhaps the most ironic thing about this flawed way of thinking is that we really do have many powers that we utterly ignore, like intuition, imagination, empathy and wisdom. Instead, we believe in a bunch of things we can't actually do like read people's minds, predict the future and fix everyone's problems. This is why I call it the Pseudo Superhero, because we only *think* we can do these amazing feats.

Alas, our Pseudo Superhero is so well meaning. It's just trying to anticipate all our problems and the problems of others, and solve them before they happen. Recognizing that these aren't your actual superpowers, will free you from hours of frustration and heartache.

Don't bother me with facts — I already know the outcome

You make a negative interpretation about the future even though there are no definitive facts to support your conclusion. This kind of thinking also involves skimming over facts and/or the process to get to a conclusion. It has a characteristic speediness.

Human beings experience time as linear. This means we don't *know* what is going to happen next, but we *think* we do. This kind of thinking leads us to believe (falsely) that we already know the outcome. For me this kind of thinking generally leaps to an unhappy ending because I genuinely believe I am omniscient.

I'm prone to be too smart for my own good and overthinking situations. I assess the situation and often arrive at a negative conclusion. The irony is that I am generally wrong. If I had a friend or colleague who had given me as much inaccurate information as I have given myself, I would stop listening to them. But, for some reason, despite my very low ratio of correct predictions, I continue to believe everything I say!

Recognizing the simple truth that I don't really know the outcome of any particular situation gives me a great deal of peace. A great exercise to combat this kind of thinking is to observe what is happening in the present moment. You can do this by bringing your attention to your own breath for a minute, and then observing what is actually happening right now. The most common experience that I have when I do this is discovering that *nothing happened*. In the here and now, everything is fine.

Antidotes
• *Notice when you are predicting the future.*
• Use the mantra "Keep Your Head where my feet are" to stay in the present moment.

ॐ

I know what you think, even if you didn't tell me

You assume that you know what someone is thinking, usually something negative, without reasonable information to support your view. You interpret others' actions and behavior as relating to something you've done.

This kind of thinking contains a degree of grandiosity because it suggests that you know things that you can't possibly know. It is based on the fear of being caught as an impostor who is profoundly flawed. It took me years to realize the simple truth that other people didn't think about me that much or that often. What I believed was a negative reaction to me was in fact, not personal.

Most of the time when people are angry, rude or impatient it has little or nothing to do with me. I used to lose my patience in traffic when people cut me off. Then one day, I realized that I cut people off when I was late or frustrated. I began to see other drivers in the same light. They didn't know me and they didn't cut me off because they were out to get me. The realization that they weren't even thinking about me allowed me to ease up and even empathize with them.

This kind of erroneous mind reading caused me innumerable problems at work and in relationships. I never bothered to check out my incorrect assumptions I just acted as if my assumptions were accurate. As I began to recover from shame, I learned to check out my false assumptions with someone I could trust. I was surprised to discover I was frequently wrong. My interpretation of people's behavior didn't match reality.

Antidotes

- *Recognize that the only thoughts you know for sure are your own.*
- *Check the objective facts.*

❧❦

I can predict what's going to happen in this situation, and it's probably going to be bad

You believe that you know the outcome of a situation will be bad. You have confidence in your ability to predict the future even when circumstances don't support your story.

We hear this often in the news, pundits

predicting the catastrophic consequences of this policy or that fashion trend. There's nothing wrong with speculating as long as you recognize that it's only speculation, not fact.

Just as we give unnecessary weight to our feelings we may be prone to give unnecessary weight to our predictions. Life is fluid and complex, things change. We don't know what's going to happen. Even when things have happened before, they are unlikely to happen exactly the same way again. Life is like a huge lottery and all of us are visited with both good and bad fortune. Making false predictions can poison many otherwise good circumstances and relationships.

Part of this thinking comes from our entertainment. Even if we are not screenwriters, we all recognize the three-act story structure in which our hero faces conflict based on some character flaw or misbehavior. We also know that somehow in the third act, the conflict will be resolved. This leads us to two troublesome conclusions; first, that life involves conflict and drama, and if there isn't drama something is wrong, and second, that we know how the story ends.

In both cases, we are wrong. Unless we live in war zone, most days don't involve drama, most days involve simple events that can be joyfully done. Also, life is a constantly unfolding story. We don't know how it will end, and we shouldn't act as if we do. So if you are going to invent an ending, why not invent a positive outcome?

Antidotes
- *Stay in the present moment.*
- *A useful mantra is "Keep your head where my feet are."*
- *Check the facts*

∂∾✑

I know the solution, so it's up to me to fix it

You feel an excessive sense of responsibility for situations you didn't cause and probably can't right. You feel compelled to intervene because you believe you know the solution, even when you weren't asked for help or advice. You think you know what other people need.

This kind of thinking can be tricky because part of participating in civil society is helping. Many of us stretch ourselves too thinly or find ourselves overwhelmed by situations we don't have the resources to solve. This is particularly acute for both perfectionists and people with leadership skills. Just because we can do something doesn't mean we should[19].

---

[19] There's that word again!

Most of us are not very good at saying "No," especially since we tie our sense of self-worth to accomplishment. At times, we may rob others of the opportunity to learn or grow because we leap in too soon. We may even irritate people or make a situation worse if we don't recognize that it's possible to be *too* helpful. Before we intervene, it can be a good habit to ask if people want help or advice. We can also interrupt our Pseudo Superhero pattern by asking what kind of help people need. It's important to note that although we may be right, our help may not be needed.

My husband and I have a long running argument about my car keys. If he finds them laying around the house, he'll pick them up and carry them into our bedroom. Occasionally he has accidentally put my keys in his pocket and left the house. There's nothing wrong with him putting my keys away if he asks me first. Putting my keys in his pocket crosses the from helpful to *too* helpful.

Antidotes
• Ask if your help is needed.
• Learn to say "No" even when you know how to do something.
• Foster a habit of self-care.

Quit Talking Dirty to Yourself

Many of us suffer from all of these forms of thinking and trying to quit all of them cold turkey would be nearly impossible. Some of these forms of thinking began almost before you could talk. These old habits can't be rooted out overnight, but it is possible to make progress. Start by identifying which habitual thoughts plague you the most.

Try listing the top three unsexy things you say to yourself here:

1.

2.

3.

When you notice any of these forms of thinking cropping up, say aloud (if possible), "I don't want to hurt myself by thinking this way." If you find this exercise helpful, in a few months tackle three more habitual thoughts and repeat the process.

My therapist gave me a list of negative thought patterns from the national bestseller, *Feeling*

Good: The New Mood Therapy[20] by David D. Burns, M.D. When I was first learning to identify my own habitual thoughts, I carried this list in my purse and found it helpful in figuring what kind of negative thought patterns I was employing. Naming things can be very powerful. Dr. Burns' book is an excellent resource for identifying and combating what he calls Cognitive Distortion. I also

Reducing any form of harmful thinking will contribute to a sense of confidence and well-being. My own experience was similar to training for a long-distance run. At first, it seemed impossible to run two miles but gradually as I trained, it became easy to run 10 miles. In the same way, you can start just trying to identify one kind of thinking. Gradually, it will become a habit to catch the multi-faceted ways that you run yourself down. Be patient — slow process of changing is already underway.

---

[20] Find this list of cognitive distortions and treatments by David D. Brown, M.D. in The Feeling Good Handbook in 1980. I highly recommend reading this book for a better understanding of negative thought patterns.

Sharks, Coyotes and Other Killer Thoughts

Over time, I've identified several kinds of negative self-talk which I think are particularly prevalent among people with eating disorders and addictions. I've shared them below along with antidotes for each kind of killer thinking.

Dog-Piling *You have a negative experience, thought or feeling and you begin piling up all the negative experiences on top of this feeling. Instead of experiencing one disappointment you aggregate them with all your disappointments.*

This painful behavior is like throwing lighter fluid on a fire to put it out. I tend to do this with things that other people say about me or to me. If someone says I have a short temper, I'll immediately begin to catalog my character defects. I'll think. "He's right and look at all the other times I've lost my temper. Plus, I'm lazy and selfish besides." Pretty soon, I have a whole festival of ways to put Stephanie down and prove how bad and defective she really is.

In my experience, this is very common among women. We are socialized to cooperate, which is a healthy social behavior. However, many women take cooperation to an extreme and become totally submissive and ashamed to speak up. We keep ourselves down with a steady stream of negative self-talk, dog piling whenever we can. Imagine what a difference it could make to root for yourself instead.

Antidotes
- *Bless yourself instead of cursing yourself.*
- *Examine the positive evidence.*
- *Be your own cheerleader*

Lionizing Others *You exaggerate the good qualities of others or make someone more heroic than they really are, thereby diminishing who you are. (The Unreliable Storyteller is helping weave this myth)*

I was always looking for a mentor to follow or a hero to save me. When I got lost, paid my bills late, forgot people's birthdays and anniversaries, I always assumed that others didn't make these normal mistakes. I thought they were all living perfect lives and I was stumbling from one disaster to the next. This problem was particularly acute with bosses. I would always assume they had never made the foolish mistakes that I made, so I tried to hide my mistakes whenever possible.

I also did this with most of the men I dated. I would imagine that they were superhuman, perfect breadwinners, patient, sensitive and smart. Soon I didn't feel worthy of their attention and began to avoid allowing the relationship to grow. I had done this in my childhood with my sister, who I imbued with a saintly nature which, by contrast, implied I was evil. All of this deadly comparative thinking led me to believe that I was simply not good enough for any job or any relationship. I went around feeling I was less than everyone else.

Like so many other kinds of flawed thinking I failed to assess the facts. I exaggerated my own negative qualities and enhanced the good qualities of others. My therapist taught me to accept and appreciate both my strengths and my weaknesses. As a result, I slowly became able to a take a more measured approach and notice those around me had both the good qualities and weaknesses. She also told me 'don't compare my insides to their outsides.'

We are likely to discount our own opinion or experience because we believe someone knows better. I have a tendency to do this with people in authority or with men. I simply assume they must be right or know more than I do. I also take on the opinions of others; if they say I'm lazy then I think it must be true.

An interesting part of my recovery is that my posture has improved. I see myself as having as much value and my opinions as having equal worth as anyone else's in the room.

Antidotes
- *Use the mantra "Neither more than nor less than"*
- *Avoid comparing yourself to others*

❧❦

Ants in the Kitchen. *You are calm and logical in crisis. You are able to manage complex projects and difficult situations with ease, particularly when in service of others. Small and ordinary situations are overwhelming and emotional. You find yourself unable to handle what seem like ordinary problems.*

A friend of mine who has an extremely visible job and managed multi-million dollar budgets couldn't get rid of the ants in her kitchen. One day she lamented that she had no problem addressing her boss who was a demanding CEO, but she was undone by the ants in her kitchen.

I suffer from this same problem. I can deal with going to the Emergency Room in the middle of the night, but when figuring out how to fix my leaking toilet seems insurmountable. Surprisingly, I've begun to recognize that this is an expression of grandiosity. I think I can and should deal with emergencies, but life's more mundane problems are not something I should have to do. I've also found that this relates to Silver Bullet thinking because I like big problems with clear solutions. Slowing down and thinking about a small problem is much harder for me.

Antidotes
- *Ask for help*
- *Use the mantra "Neither more than nor less than"*
- *Use the mantra "This too shall pass."*

᚛᚜

Silver Bullet Thinking *The idea that life can be clean, organized and orderly if you could just find the perfect solution for every problem. This kind of thinking is characterized by a kind of once-and-done mentality. You believe that most of the problems in life have a single, permanent, perfect solution. (Warning: The Deluded Despot is on hand.)*

I still struggle with this kind of thinking. I desperately want life to be neat and orderly. I want my kitchen to stay clean, my car to stay full of gas, my bills to be paid *all the time.* For these everyday occurrences, I want to figure out how to get them done once and for all. This kind of thinking suggests that once I solve a problem, I should never have to solve it again.

I first noticed this thinking when I was recovering from my eating disorders. When my therapist identified a particular behavior, I wanted her to tell me how to stop, and then I wanted to *never do it again.* The recovery from eating disorders is a slow process full of ups and downs. I often liken it to the game Whack-A-Mole. When one behavior stops another pops its head up. I would over eat, then starve, then diet, then over-exercise, then count calories, and then over-eat again. Progress is far from linear. Over time I've adopted strategies to deal with different problems. I don't eat seconds which helps with overeating. I have other techniques to prevent me from skipping meals. But it still happens, sometimes I overeat, sometimes I skip meals and hope that I'll drop five pounds in one afternoon. This is what progress looks like for me today.

This kind of once-and-for-all thinking existed everywhere in my life. It oversimplifies life and doesn't allow for change or unexpected complications. I am forever vowing to myself, 'I'll never do that again.'

What I have learned is this: Knowing you have a head cold doesn't cure it. I still have to rest, drink fluids and take cold medicine. More to the point, once I recover from a head cold, it doesn't mean I'll never get one again. This is the nature of life; it is cyclical and iterative. My lifelong desire to solve every problem once and for all doesn't change this simple fact. Acceptance of this truth has made life easier.

Antidotes
- *Develop acceptance.*
- *Use the mantra "Life on life's terms" or "Progress not perfection."*

❧❧

Monday Morning Thinking. *The idea that you'll start the new diet/ program/class tomorrow and from then on, everything will go perfectly.*

This is the way we think every time we start a new diet, "today may not be perfect, *but tomorrow....*" This kind of thinking has at its root the idea that there will be some perfect day or week, that if we could just start out right we'll get what we want. The catch is what we really want is contentment, thinking that tomorrow will be perfect is not likely to make us content with the present moment.

Monday Morning Thinking also fuels the tendency to see the world as black-and-white. On Sunday afternoon, I'll eat all the ice cream and brownies I want but starting Monday, my diet will be perfect. The truth is that life is not neatly divided into perfect days and imperfect days. Some days I might make mistakes, some days I might not. "Life," as my husband says, "is shit and sugar on the same spoon."

• *Try making small changes in your habits instead of big sweeping ones.*
• *Allow for gray areas in your thinking.*
• *Be gentle with yourself.*
• *Start the change right now.*

❧❧

Eastbound Fixation *This is the thought that you will get a particular outcome from a particular thought or behavior even if there's no evidence to support that view. It's the idea that heading east (or whatever crazy idea you have that doesn't work) is the only and best solution.*

The example I use to explain this is that in order to get to Hawaii I need to board a plane and fly west. If I get on a train that's traveling east, I'm not going to get to Hawaii, no matter how hard I try or what I believe. I just can't help myself, no matter where I want to go I'm fixated on going East. It doesn't mean there's anything wrong with trains, it just means it won't get me to the desired destination.

This is a kind of thinking that can be combated by asking for help. Find someone who has overcome your struggle and ask them what they did. I am consistently surprised how often what others suggest is the exact opposite of what I think I should do. I've also found what works is often simpler than any idea I had.

Especially during my most anorexic years, I would try to control my eating by saying cruel things to myself, which never worked. Beating myself up was my Eastbound Fixation. Once I started to recover, I realized the road to recovery required being gentle with myself.

Antidotes
- *Try something new or different.*
- *Explore alternatives.*
- *Ask for help.*

かがや

Coyote Fallacy *This is thinking too much about everything. Like the coyote in the roadrunner cartoons, you come up with clever ideas that only hurts you. You are just too smart for your own good.*

Similar to the Eastbound Fixation, the Coyote Fallacy is a flawed view of cause and effect. The coyote is the trickster of Native American lore who is forever trying to outsmart all the other creatures usually to his own detriment. He always chooses a convoluted, though clever, plan to get what he wants instead of relating to the other creatures in a straight-forward way.

For years, I believed that if I would only lose weight I'd be happy. Along the way I did hundreds of crazy things, like starving for days on end, that only resulted in *un*happiness. This kind of thinking was particularly deadly for me because I would concoct complicated, time-consuming plans that never achieved the desired goal and ultimately wasted energy that could've been put to better use.

A classic example of my Coyote Fallacy Thinking was to practice volleyball until my knees were red and swollen and I could barely stand. I wanted to try out for my college team. I spent more time in the gym than the women who had made the team and probably accomplished less. There is a normal, healthy level of practice to acquire mastery but I went way beyond that. The idea was to advance my skills as quickly as possible, regardless of the consequences to my body. I injured myself repeatedly and ultimately had to have two knee surgeries. I'm no longer able to play volleyball at all because of the damage I did to my own body.

Notice how the coyote was always out in the desert by himself concocting his schemes, then BAM he got hit in the head with an anvil he never saw coming. These are two of the main characteristics of the Coyote Fallacy. First, we're obsessed with the outcome like the coyote who just wanted to eat the roadrunner. Second, we're making these plans on own. I often notice I'm on the Coyote Fallacy track when my idea seems urgent, my thoughts are rigid or I want to do something without checking in with another person.

This kind of thinking often turns up when I have to do something I consider to be either ordinary or tedious. I am forever trying to figure out a faster, smarter way to file my taxes or complete a project at work. Some things just take as long as they take.

Antidotes

•*Check with another person before you enact your grand plan*
•*Ask yourself if you making something too complicated*
•*Pause before you act*

෨ஒ

Special Person Exemption *You think you know how to beat the system or you think you don't need to do what others have to do. You believe you're exempt because your circumstances are special.*

This applies to feeling I don't need to abide by the rules others abide by like, it's okay for me to speed. I don't have to pay my taxes by the deadline. I don't have to stand in that line. This usually results in manufacturing excuses or trying to talk my way out of problems. I complained to a friend once when I got a speeding ticket and she replied, "I'm sorry you got a ticket, but I speed almost every day, don't you? You're kind of lucky you only got one." Her comment uncovered a profound truth, most of the time we aren't held accountable for the things we do. The fact is the Highway Patrol could stop me almost every day on the freeway and they'd be justified. Trying to wiggle out of a ticket is denying the simple truth that I am responsible for my choices. I'm not special, mostly I'm lucky.

Whenever I catch myself thinking I know better than other people, or I'm exempt, I know I'm in trouble. There are seven deadly words that are a sure sign of the Special Person Exemption, "You don't understand, my case is different" Whenever I catch myself thinking this way I try to combat it by recognizing the rules apply to me too.

The main problem with this kind of thinking is it builds the muscle of grandiosity and creates an environment for selfishness to grow. Developing a sense of humility and ordinariness is a powerful way to recognize that we are all struggling and suffering in the same way as everyone else. Our experience in life isn't that different from anyone else's.

Antidotes
• *Use the mantra "One among many."*
• *Embrace being ordinary.*
• *Ask yourself how the rules DO apply to you, stand in line (either figuratively or actually) or let someone go in front of you.*
• *Try using 'please' and 'thank you'.*

Jumping the Shark. *You find something that works well for you and then you take it too far. If one is good, 100 is better. You find yourself unable to stop repeating the same behavior, even when you know you've gone too far.*

Jumping the Shark[21] is a term used in Hollywood to describe when a TV show or a movie begins to decline in its evolution. It originated when the Fonz literally jumped over a shark on the popular 80s show *Happy Days*. Critics felt that Happy Days had once been a clever, funny show and that jumping the shark was just too far.

This is exactly what I do. I take something that is a healthy instinct and carry it too far. I like to have things organized and neat. I label drawers and containers to make it easier to remember where things are put away. Labeling my own drawers might be a little excessive, labeling my husband's drawers is Jumping the Shark. It's important to notice this kind of thinking is usually born from a good idea or something that's working. Sometimes all that's necessary is to dial it back a little. This kind of thinking is innate to perfectionists because we are always trying to top ourselves or make improvements. We want to do a little better or a little more.

---

[21] According to Wikipedia it was popularized by radio personality John Hein in the 1990's

I am especially prone to this with my time. I just keep wedging in a few more things to do until I'm exhausted. Managing and over-managing my time leads me to feeling overwhelmed. The fear of missing out on something can also be a form of this kind of thinking. I need to recognize doing many fun, exciting things can be good but it can also be too much. I can notice that resting might be the best thing for me.

Antidotes
- *Use the mantra "I have enough. I do enough. I am enough."*
- *Notice when the idea of MORE comes up.*

❧❦

The Immortal Bond Thinking *You believe the current situation is permanent and unchangeable. You find yourself feeling like a victim in a particular circumstance that you believe you cannot escape. You fear making a decision because you believe you may have to live with it forever or that you are forever trapped by some past decision.*

This often comes up for me with jobs. People often use the term 'Golden Handcuffs' but what they actually mean is that they have created a personal Immortal Bond. I once accepted a job working for a big corporation in part because I believed it would look good on my resume. Very shortly after I started work I realized that the culture was poisonous and all my co-workers were all extremely unhappy. I stayed in the job because I was afraid of the consequences of leaving. One day I told a friend how unhappy I was and she said. "What would it take for you to be happy?" I realized that I hadn't even allowed to think about looking for another job because I believed I was stuck. I started to imagine the environment that I wanted instead of focusing on the difficulty of the existing situation. Gradually, my thinking began to shift, I started to see that I had a choice and I could look for a new job. After a year, a colleague at another company called to offer a perfect job. The Immortal Bond was only in my head.

I also find myself paralyzed when I have to make decisions. I believe that every decision is a gateway that will lead to either the perfect outcome or a disaster. Notice how this is related to Unreliable Storyteller, spinning up a story about an outcome I can't possibly know. When I had to buy a new car I tormented myself with the enormity of the decision. I researched every possible model, feature and style. I test drove multiple cars and waffled back and forth. Once I finally bought a car I continued to think about the resale value and wondered if I made the best choice. Then one day I realized I'd created an Immortal Bond with my car. It's totally fine to sell my car and buy a new one any time.

Antidotes
- *Use the mantra "This too shall pass."*
- *Consider the third alternative.*
- *Notice when something feels permanent.*

∂∽∂

The Post-Post-Game Syndrome

You negatively evaluate your performance, your conversations or your appearance after the event is over. You try to find ways to improve for next time. Sometimes you issue apologies[22] after the fact for things (often minor) that you said or did.

I'm a big sports fan, and like most sports fans I like to watch the post-game show. I enjoy hearing what the commentators have to say about important plays and key players in the game. So, I say this with love and respect, the post-game is kind of silly. Think about it, the game is over, we all just watched it, we can't change the outcome and yet we spend hours talking about it. You know what would be sillier than that? Talking *about the post-game.* Imagine if after the post-game show, I sat around and talked about the way the commentator talked about the game after the game. This is the Post-Post-Game Syndrome. We go out and live our lives, then we talk about our lives and then we go home and evaluate how

---

[22] See the chapter *Boycott Apologies* for details on when and how to apologize

we did at living our lives and talking about our lives. This situation creates a never-ending loop where we aren't present for the moment. We are always weighing and evaluating and commentating about the past. We miss the key play because we're still talking about *talking about* the last game.

I was invited to a movie screening and after-party with a friend I seldom saw. We had a wonderful time seeing movie stars and snacking at a fancy hotel restaurant. We sat at the bar and enjoyed a long, rambling conversation about our lives, our families and some of our difficult mornings. I went home feeling the satisfaction of getting to attend a special event and connecting in a real way with another human being.

As I pulled out of the parking lot, I received a text from my friend. "Sorry about that lame comment about the Simpsons. Failed attempt at humor. Hope you don't think I'm a total idiot." As soon as she had gone to her car, she had begun to evaluate what she said in the bar and determine how I might feel about it. I replied to my friend. "I had a wonderful time. I hope we can do it again soon." What I wanted to say is how sad I was that she had indulged in this kind of painful thinking, I know this behavior so well, I've done it for years. The trouble is that I always found myself lacking. My potent inner critic never gave me a good review. This the same thing that happened to my friend.

I've confide in my mentor when I've experience this kind of Post-Post-Game Syndrome and I've observed that she is masterful at being kind to herself. Often, when I tell her the saga of my supposedly silly mistake she says, "Well, glad that's over!" Hearing her say it reminds me I have the choice and the freedom to move on. Mistakes happen, I don't have to stay stuck there commentating on the event after it's over.

Antidotes

• Use the mantra "Well, glad that's over" or "It's safe to let it go."
• Boycott apologies.
• Give up the post-game game and stay in the present.

෨෨෨

Try making a list of all of the killer thoughts and carry it around with you. Whenever you catch yourself employing one of these forms of thinking just put a make a little tick next to it. In a very short time you'll start to notice patterns in the ways you think. Don't try to do this perfectly. This is fieldwork. You're just gathering data to try to understand your habitual behavior with more clarity.

After a few days our list might look like this:

DOG-PILING III

LIONIZING OTHERS)

ANTS IN THE KITCHEN))))))

SILVER-BULLET THINKING))))))))))))

MONDAY MORNING THINKING)))

EASTBOUND FIXATION)

COYOTE FALLACY)

SPECIAL PERSON EXEMPTION))))))))

JUMPING THE SHARK)

IMMORTAL BOND)))

POST-POST-GAME))

You'll start to identify the most common forms of thinking and notice patterns. In my case, it's Silver-Bullet Thinking, Monday Morning Thinking and Special Person Exemption. Next, look up the antidotes for your top three and try using them for 21 days.

Use the universal antidote, *I don't want to hurt myself by thinking this way,* or pick out one or two mantras that are specific to your particular killer thinking. The key is to want to be kind to yourself and begin to develop a healthy way of viewing the world around you.

Firing the Committee

There's an old saying "A camel is a horse designed by a committee." Although committees serve a purpose in some environments, equally as often they arrive at wrong- headed and insufficient conclusions. This is the kind of committee that took up residence inside my head. They were a malicious collection of naysayers whose objectives were unclear and whose actions were at best self-serving. I allowed them to rule me for years and what was worse, I didn't even realize they were there.

My friend described her committee as a group of bumbling Peter Sellers' Inspector Clouseau's wandering around aimlessly and consistently arriving at the wrong conclusion. I always pictured my committee as group of graying Patricians who would never allow themselves to crack a joke or express any kind of happiness, excitement or joy.

My committee was omnipresent and diligent. No matter what I did they were always ready to evaluate or correct. After having a brief social conversation, they would grill me mercilessly, "Why did you say that?" or "Why are you so awkward?" or pass immediate judgments like "I'm sure they didn't like you" or "You always sound so desperate." This steady stream of criticism was so natural to my way of thinking that I barely noticed it. As I grew up, I incorporated their withering criticism as a part of my every day thinking. It never occurred to me to think any other way, until my friend and I talked about our experiences with the mean voices inside our head.

Our conversations helped me become aware of the constant banter of this unproductive committee. They seemed to think that their corrections and suggestions made me a better person but, in fact, they just made me self-conscious and fearful. As time went on, I went from being aware of their presence, to mild annoyance, to outright hostility. My friend and I decided we were sick and tired of our committees and that they were going to be fired. I spent a few weeks writing down every single thing the committee said to me. Here's a sample of a few of the things they said:

You are incompetent and they are going to find out.

You are so emotional it makes other people uncomfortable.

You'll never have any real success.

No one will ever really love you as you are.

You scare people away.

You're not allowed to express negative emotions.

You can never cry or show weakness.

Sadly, this list went on for several pages. Seeing the committees' conclusions in black-and-white made me acutely aware of how painful these messages really were. It also pointed out how essentially pointless they were. It didn't serve me to have a personal sense of defeat as a constant tape in my head. It fueled a relentless perfectionism because no matter what I did it was never good enough for the committee. They always wanted a little more than I could give.

On the day that the committee was set to be fired, I called my mentor and asked her if I could read the list of the committee's pronouncements to her before I fired them. I read the whole long list to her and at the end she let a short, soft "oh." The hopelessness and sadness of that word has never left me. I realized that the cruelty I had inflicted on myself was both painful and almost incomprehensible to her. I was able for a split second to touch the tenderness in my own heart, to feel the utter sadness of a life spent in blistering self-criticism and perfectionism. Then I burned the list. They were gone. I'm sure it wasn't just that one action, I'm sure it was the therapy and the other personal work I had done to heal my eating disorders that helped. For the first time in my life I was able to live without the fear of the relentless, exhausting criticism inside my head. At the same time, I had adopted the mantra, "I have enough, I do enough, I am enough." I know it helped me to repeat this regularly when I felt the committee's criticism rising up. My friend fired her committee by escorting them to popular pub where they play the song "My Heart Will Go On" continuously day and night and she left them there. For years afterwards, whenever I would think of my committee I would think of all my friend's Inspector Clouseaus sitting in a pub listening to the same song over and over and wondering what they could do to escape. I always felt that they received their just punishment.

It is difficult to root out the committee. Discovering their presence is an excellent first step. Noticing their negative banter and the way they make you feel insufficient or unworthy is a good starting point. For most people, it's a longtime habit and breaking it is not likely to happen overnight. I found meditation to be an invaluable tool in beginning to recognize these negative thought patterns and releasing them. It also helps to notice the essential inaccuracy of their pronouncements. I continued to believe I was unlovable for years after I married a man who clearly loved me. Trying to get rid of the committee on your own is difficult. If you try this, I suggest working with a trusted friend, mentor or therapist. Before you expose this very vulnerable side of yourself, be sure that the person you confide in will not make you feel worse. They should have a track record of being gentile, loving and non-judgmental.

Subsequent to firing my committee, I created a list of positive affirmations. A good starting point is using the list of what the committee says and then writing down the opposite. I made this list, transferred the ones I liked best (or felt I needed the most) to index cards which I carry in my purse. I pull them out and read them aloud when I had a spare moment. Over time my thought patterns have become more positive. I essentially reprogrammed myself to use positive thoughts instead of the negative thoughts. Here's a sample of a few of them:

I am able to do things well when I set my mind to it.

I am loveable.

I am highly creative.

I am resourceful.

All of these things are true, but I never allowed myself to see them because I was so busy listening to the committee.

You become what your mind is occupied with, so why not fill it with positive ideas about yourself? I have observed that highly successful and competent people have a positive assessment of themselves. Can you imagine Michael Phelps, Tom Brady or Serena Williams saying "I'm not that good I'm just fooling people"? Expressing a sane evaluation of yourself is not arrogance. As discussed in the earlier chapter thinking more than or less than oneself contributes to pride and self-centered thinking. A sane assessment of who you are and what you value will build self-confidence, compassion and gentleness toward others.

Don't worry, I can tell you from experience you have nothing to fear. I thought if I fired my committee I would slip into a lazy, sloppy lifestyle. It turns out I am still able to be punctual, accurate and excellent without my committee pushing me. In fact, my experience has been that I am better at doing things without them than I was with their exhausting criticism. Firing them is one of the most empowering and positive things I have done in my adult life.

"I'm Fine" and Other Half Truths

I grew up in an environment where we did not talk about our feelings very much. I remember being anxious and fearful as a child and feeling that it wasn't acceptable to express these negative feelings. I believe this is a common experience for eldest children who often become oriented toward achievement and approval. My maternal grandmother was a very tough survivor. She had lived through the Great Depression, the early sudden death of her husband and years of single parenthood in an era when working mothers were uncommon. She had a low tolerance for complaints and for people that couldn't "hike themselves up by their bootstraps" and "get on with it." I internalized this deeply. At some point, I adopted the point-of-view that emotions were a problem. I felt the need to maintain a very narrow range of emotional expression which ranged from okay to moderately happy.

By the time I was in my forties, I had winnowed my emotions down to just a few. I knew when I was happy, when I was angry, when I was afraid and when I was sad. I had no sense of nuanced emotions. I also had a hard time figuring what, if anything, I could do to modulate my feelings. Around this time, I had a friend who explained to me that feelings where much more complex than happy or sad. It sounds amazing to me now but at the time it was a revelation. She gave me a list to help me identify my feelings. She hand-wrote additional feelings on the list and added an incredibly helpful inscription which said, "Where do you feel these?" I soon learned about a field of study called somatic psychology. It is a technique that teaches patients to uncover their emotional reactions by connecting with the physical experience of their feelings. Until my friend pointed this out, I never realized my emotions had connection to parts of my body. The most common and universal example is that most human beings feel love at their heart center. This is what somatic psychology endeavors to uncover.

I used the following list as a guide to help me become acquainted with a wider variety of feelings. I found it helpful to look up the dictionary definition of some of these words. For example, I didn't really know the difference between 'sensual' and 'sexual'. When I felt a feeling, I would pull out the list and ask myself, what best describes how I am feeling?

This is an opportunity for more field work. Observe your feelings, spend two minutes sitting quietly and ask yourself, "How do I feel?" Then, I'd like to invite you to do something I think is *crazy*, get out a pen (*not a pencil*) and add a few feelings of your own. (Yeah, I know, writing in a book *in pen!* What if you want to erase it later? What if you add it to the wrong list or misspell it? What if you run out of space? Notice all these thoughts. They *are* perfectionism.) The important this is that there is no right answer, you just feel the way you feel. Make up your own words if you need to. Feelings are utterly personal, only you will ever truly know how you feel.

I have offered both physical and emotional feelings because for me I wasn't very good at defining either one. This list of words helped to spur me on to think more deeply and to connect with the physical experience in my body. For example, I learned that anxiety made me feel nauseous and I experienced it almost daily. Recognizing anxiety helped me to see that I needed tools to cope with it. I also found that identifying more-nuanced emotions made me able to cope with them better. Realizing the difference between feeling vulnerable and feeling sad allowed me to use discretion about putting myself in difficult situations.

One of the most surprising conclusions was what my friend Alex calls the 'double dipper feelings.' I never knew that, like a double dip ice cream, I could feel multiple distinct and separate emotions at the same time. I could feel sad and grateful at the precise same moment. I could be angry at my husband and also longing for him to love me. It was a powerful lesson to learn that it is possible to allow multiple and sometimes conflicting emotions at the same time. I began to realize that my compulsion to eat, starve or throw-up was the result of a desire to stamp out these complex, powerful and frequently ignored emotions. With time, I found it interesting to study the variety of emotions and my physical response to them. Anger is a kind of rising heat that started at my heart center and rose to my head. Fear is a nervous flutter in my stomach and fast heartbeat. Gratitude is warmth that pervades my whole body. Eventually, I became a connoisseur of complex emotions. I sampled them and allowed them to be present without the need to remove or fix them. It was an exciting new inward voyage. The main discovery I made was emotions are fine; they are a part of the human experience and don't necessarily require action. I learned to identify them and enjoy the wild ride. Like watching a spectacular storm, I could watch them arise, roil and subside without any action required on my part.

Emotional Feelings Menu

1. Abandoned
2. Afraid
3. Angry
4. Annoyed
5. Anxious
6. Apathetic
7. Appreciated
8. Arrogant
9. Ashamed
10. Bored
11. Cherished
12. Compassionate
13. Defiant
14. Depressed
15. Disappointed
16. Empty
17. Excited
18. Faceless
19. Forgotten
20. Frustrated
21. Gratitude
22. Grieving
23. Happy
24. Hurt
25. Indifferent
26. Irritated
27. Isolated
28. Joyous
29. Lonely
30. Longing
31. Loved
32. Loving

33. Mad
34. Nervous
35. Numb
36. Open
37. Peaceful
38. Prideful
39. Proud
40. Raw
41. Rejected
42. Resistant
43. Righteous
44. Sad
45. Self-pity
46. Self-justified
47. Strong
48. Tense
49. Terrified
50. Victimized
51. Vulnerable
52. Wanting
53. Willful
54. Withdrawn
55. Wronged
57.
58.
59.
60.
61.
62.
63.
64.

Physical Feelings Menu

1. Achy
2. Afraid
3. Agitated
4. Brittle
5. Cold
6. Contracted
7. Comfortable
8. Craving
9. Dense
10. Disembodied
11. Energetic
12. Energized
13. Endangered
14. Exhausted
15. Exposed
16. Fatigued
17. Feverish
18. Full
19. Headachy
20. Hot
21. Hungry
22. Hyper
23. Injured
24. Jittery
25. Lazy
26. Lethargic
27. Nauseous
28. Numb
29. Pained
30. Paralyzed
31. Prickly
32. Restless
33. Relaxed
34. Satisfied

34. Sensual
35. Sexual
36. Sick
37. Sleepy
38. Sore
39. Spacious
40. Spent
41. Starving
42. Stuffed
43. Sweaty
44. Tense
45. Tight
46. Tired
47. Thirsty
48. Trapped
49. Wanting
50. Warm
51.
52.
53.
54.
55
56.
57
58.
59.
60.
61.
62.
63.
64.

Stop Being Fine and Get Real

When my mom was being hospitalized with cancer, I spent nearly every day in the hospital; I ate poorly, and hardly slept and was paralyzed with anxiety and fear. This is when I noticed my tendency to try to control my feelings to make others comfortable. When someone asked me how I was I'd answer 'fine,' which clearly wasn't true. I was whatever the opposite of fine is.

The problem wasn't saying 'I'm fine', it was trying to *be fine* so that others wouldn't be uncomfortable. For years, I did this with uncomfortable emotions. I tried not to be angry, impatient or sad. I believed no one would like me if I expressed those emotions.

There are two important things I learned about this habit. First, feelings aren't good or bad. Being sad doesn't mean there's something wrong with me. Second, not expressing the full range of feelings makes me inauthentic. If I don't show up as an honest authentic person I'm not able to be vulnerable. Vulnerability is the way that we connect to each another so when I don't share real feelings I don't develop meaningful bonds with other human beings.

Context is important. I don't need to make myself vulnerable to the checker at the grocery store, and don't need to go around spewing my feelings at other people. It means I need to acknowledge how I'm feeling within myself. When my mom was sick, I didn't need to tell everyone I met that I was sad, tired, frustrated, and scared, but I did need to know what was going on inside of me. When a close friend asked how I was doing, I'd say, "I'm so tired I can hardly think" or "I'm afraid my mom is going to die." This was an honest reflection of who I was in that moment. Most of my friends were asking because they sincerely wanted to know.

Another mistake I often made was trying to craft my feelings to how I thought I *should* feel. When I bought my first house I thought I *should* be happy and excited but in fact I was scared and anxious about the future. Because I didn't allow myself to acknowledge my fears I didn't talk to my husband about how nervous I felt about missing a mortgage payment. It was a missed opportunity to build intimacy in the early years of our marriage and I could have been comforted by sharing the burden with him.

Meditation is very useful tool in learning to ride emotions. Mindfulness is an excellent way to handle strong, painful or conflicting emotions[23].

---

[23]Dzogchen Ponlop Rinpoche has written an excellent book and recorded a series of talks the subject of emotions, for details on this collection see the reference section of the book.

The Buddhist teacher Ponlop Rinpoche likens emotions to powerful waves coming ashore. It doesn't make sense to stand on the shore waiting for the waves to crush me. Standing on a cliff at a safe distance and watching, on the other hand, can be a spectacular, memorable experience.

Through meditation I made another important revelation about my emotions. I generated them on my own. My thoughts and my story lines would spin into a storm of emotions, particularly if I fed them with additional stories. Like watching a hurricane develop on a satellite feed I could see how one event would trigger a feeling and then I would begin to wrap that with other similar events or stories. Soon I would have a powerful eye surrounded by arms of other stories headed right for me. I learned that just as I had the power to create these storms I had the power to diffuse them. By watching my emotions and the associated physical feelings I gradually became able to manage them. I realized that I wasn't angry at a co-worker, I was just tired and the confluence of events was contributing to a feeling of anger that I didn't need to act on. What I really needed was rest. This is not to discount the genuine experience of pain and joy that occurs in life. Losing a loved one is deeply painful, the birth of a child is joyful and these things should be experienced to the fullest. The trick is to watch the ways in which you inflate these feelings or exaggerate the emotional experience by adding stories to them. I tended to engage in a kind of picking at emotional scabs instead of letting them heal over naturally. Recognizing the ways in which we contribute to our own emotional state can be both a relief and a powerful tool.

Perhaps the most important discovery is that feelings are not a problem. Strong emotions don't need to be feared or removed. By finally allowing myself to feel my feelings, I discovered that they passed quickly and, even if I cried or screamed aloud, they weren't harmful. I also found that people around me were able to handle my emotions. My old thinking was that if I expressed my feelings, especially negative ones, people wouldn't like me. It is true that some people will not like my feelings but generally the people who really love and support me are able to make space for my anger, anxiety and sadness. If you don't feel there are people who are able to support you and allow the breadth of your emotions, make a conscious effort to find people who will. There are enlightened, gentle, loving people everywhere if you aspire to bring them into your life you will find them or they will find you. By offering others the freedom to feel and express the full spectrum of their feelings without judgment you will discover a new richness and depth in your relationship to others.

I read an article about the neurology of human emotion. I was surprised to discover that the duration of emotion at the occurrence of event is only 90 seconds. We use our imagination and our storytelling skills to keep the emotion alive or increase its intensity. I first experimented with this idea when I was trying to stop eating sugar. I thought, "If I only crave sugar for 90 seconds, maybe I can just wait it out." To my amazement it was true, the reason I kept craving sugar was because I whipped up a good reason to eat it or I imagined something that sounded irresistible. If I directed my attention somewhere else, I stopped craving it. Soon, I expanded this to other emotions and began to experience a sense of not being dominated by my emotions. I felt them for 90 seconds and then went on with what I was doing, if they came up again I noticed them for another 90 seconds and carried on again. Soon I discovered that even intense emotions didn't last long and I didn't need to fear them.

There are some things that are not feelings. Women often say "I feel fat", but fat is not a feeling. What they mean is that they don't feel well, strong or in control of my diet. Try to be specific about how you feel and avoid these kinds of general descriptions. Instead of feeling fat you can say that you ate too much or that you feel like you need a walk. Another example is feeling like a fraud. Fraud isn't a feeling. Instead you may feel insecure, afraid or ashamed. If you can't locate where you feel the feeling in your body you may need to dig deeper until you can.

I encourage you to explore all the dimensions of

your feelings. Notice the wealth of experience available through your physical and emotional feelings and embrace yourself as you are.

The Good Girl Dilemma

I am the eldest child and the first-born grandchild on both sides of my family. For the first 3 years of my life I was often the center of attention. Very early in life, I acquired the habit of performing for approval and trying to be good. If I was punished, which was rare, I never felt defiant I just felt sorry for failing which caused me to redouble my efforts to be good.

It wasn't long before I developed a habit of assessing what other people wanted and trying to deliver it. I became a first-class people pleaser. As long as I got approval I felt I was doing okay. The slightest inference that there was an alternative course of action or criticism caused me to be defensive or to retreat. Because my dad was working full-time and going to school I was particularly fixated on getting his approval whenever he was around, which was rare. Looking back, I see the desperation of a child trying to satisfy an adult who was probably exhausted and overwhelmed most of the time. The more I tried to get attention from the adults in my life and failed, the harder I tried. I gradually developed a belief system in which my self-esteem was based on how good I was. Determining if I was good enough depended on my subjective judgment of how much approval I got and, as a perfectionist, I just kept raising the bar.

As I grew older I added new dimensions to my rules about being a good girl. Good girls didn't go to rock concerts, ride motorcycles, smoke pot, or have sex with boys. As a teenager, I was probably more uptight than most parents. In the changing social environment of the '60s and '70s, I was something of an anomaly among my peers. I excluded myself from innocent explorations that are a normal part of growing up. The first time I ever kissed a boy I was so ashamed I couldn't sleep and I was embarrassed to look anyone in the eye for days. I decided to wait until marriage to have intercourse, but the truth was I wanted to put off having sex as long as possible. I was already estranged from my body, and accustomed to ignoring my natural instincts, so avoiding sex was a natural conclusion. I was also profoundly uncomfortable with my femininity. Gradually, my self-esteem depended almost entirely on how good I was. My natural proclivity towards competitiveness added to this. I didn't just want to be good, I wanted to be the *best* good girl.

To reinforce my natural way of thinking, society still supported a view that women were either virgins or whores. As far as I knew, there was no middle ground. Bad girls had sex. Good girls didn't. The BEST girls definitely didn't. If I did feel any kind of curiosity, physical attraction or sexual tension I felt deeply ashamed and chastised myself to being weak and bad. This turned my teenage years into a pressure cooker of constantly trying to keep a lid on what were the normal emotions and sensations of maturing. I compensated for this by adopting the role of being the wise, sensible friend. I frequently offered advice on subjects I knew nothing about and I genuinely believed I knew best. I even adopted an attitude of being superior to some of my friends who struggled because they had slept with their boyfriends or moved from relationship to relationship. The irony now is that I envy some of these girls for the breadth of their experience. I wish I had tried some of the things that they tried. It would have been appropriate behavior when I was thirteen, but not when I'm older. I have noticed that the women I know who experimented more and were wilder in their youth seem to be more settled and confident in middle-age. Of course, I can't replay my youth but I am willing to acknowledge now that I could have loosened up a bit.

At the center of my thinking about being good was this very simple syllogism:

Being good equals approval

Approval equals being loved

Therefore, being good equals being loved

As with many syllogisms, there is a flaw in my thesis and my conclusion. I spent years in pursuit of love via being good. When coupled with my perfectionism and my eating disorders, my interior pursuit became an obsession with being thin, being pretty and being well liked. I measured my sense of well-being based on how other people responded to me. I engaged in constant competition with others because I couldn't generate self-esteem on my own. It never really occurred to me that people were liked for other characteristics such as friendliness or kindness. Ironically, my best friend was well liked because she was gentle, kind and thoughtful, but I didn't make the connection until many years later. I also had a tendency to confuse self-respect with arrogance. If another girl felt good about herself I would label her 'stuck-up' and dismiss the people who liked her as deluded. On reflection, I wish I had the sense to learn how these girls fostered self-respect instead of minimizing them with my judgments.

I still live in my hometown and occasionally see some of these girls as adults. There is one in particular who I remember in elementary school as confident and self-possessed. She has always been attractive but today I recognize that in addition her natural physical endowments she feels good about herself. She has always looked people in the eye when she talks and expressed interest in others. She is at ease with being her and that's what makes her attractive. At ten years old, she understood that my syllogism had a false conclusion. The key to being loved is to love yourself.

Here's the dilemma of being a good girl. Being

good means following the rules, rules whose origins are outside of me. I can never really become my authentic self if I spend all of my time trying to shape my behavior to some outside standard, especially if the standard is wrong for me. In fact, I preclude the possibility of discovering what's right for me by fixating on the rules.

A big part of being authentic is recognizing who I really am. What I have found is that self-discovery comes when I am willing to depart from the rules. I have often experienced a feeling of tension between what I really want and what the rules say. The dilemma is that being good doesn't make me more loveable it just fuels a sense of shame. In the depths of shame, we can't experience any kind of meaningful love and we don't make a connection between our pursuit of *being good* and our failure to *feel good.*

Only when I started to meditate did I began to discover the nature of my own mind. I began to see the ways in which I was motivated by fear, reluctant to ask for help and driven by a constant sense of impatience. I've also seen my innate generosity, my willingness to help others and my natural creativity. Recognizing my own habitual patterns has made it possible for me to begin to move towards a more authentic way of life.

One of the primary ways to eliminate shame is to be authentic and it is almost impossible to be a good girl and be authentic at the same time. The good girl is almost always oriented toward sublimating her own wishes in order to perform what others' wishes, or *perceived* wishes, are. Paradoxically, many of us do things because we believe we know what others want but our perception is inaccurate or ill-informed.

Many years ago, I had a friend who was a skydiver. She started skydiving as a way to face her fear and to try doing something that she thought she could never do. Initially, she experienced a sense of release at the thrill of jumping and she continued to jump for some time. Then, she witnessed an experienced skydiver having a terrible debilitating accident. A few weeks, later a friend was killed while skydiving. Both times she called me to talk about her paralyzing fear and her desire to stop skydiving. After the death of her friend I asked her if she enjoyed skydiving. She said that she didn't enjoy it and that in fact she had wanted to stop ever since her first dive, but she felt like she had to keep going or her friends would be disappointed. She had made up a rule, she was trying to be a good girl but she wasn't being true to herself. She was terrifying herself and risking her life to carry on with some perceived set of expectations that may not have even existed. As soon as she stopped skydiving she felt a sense of relief and peace.

We are social animals and we govern ourselves by assessing what is acceptable behavior to our peers. Look at your life and notice the hundreds of rules that govern what you do. There's a value system in place at home, at your office and in society at large. There are also expected roles for your gender, your birth order, your social class and the region you live in. If you tallied up all the rules you have to follow it would be a dizzying array of conflicting expectations. Occasionally we are directly confronted by these incongruities, but most of the time we sail along trying to conform to what is expected.

When I take a moment and really examine the way I'm trying to be happy it isn't that hard to see the flaws in my logic. I am trying to be happy by doing what others expect of me. The likelihood that what my boss, or my husband, or my friend, or my mother wants is what will make me happy is very slim. The person best informed to understand what will make me genuinely happy is *me*. This doesn't mean I need to embark on a selfish mission of only making myself happy but it does mean I need to know myself.

In ancient times the Greeks went to the Oracle at Delphi to discover the truth and seek guidance for the future. 'Know Thyself' was inscribed on the wall at the entry of the Temple of Apollo in Delphi, as if self-knowledge were a precursor for greater understanding. Knowing yourself is the gateway to authenticity, and living in an authentic way will lead to genuine happiness. Being authentic is a lifelong project which requires a degree of vigilance. We encounter situations almost daily where it is not possible or not appropriate to be completely authentic.

We can't say we are bored in an important business meeting or tell our blowhard neighbor to drop dead. Society at large requires that we sometimes withhold our real feelings. However, it is vital that we create an environment where we can be authentic, whether we're alone, with a spouse or a friend we need to be able to allow ourselves our real feelings. This means being able to say what you really believe, to feel free to succeed or fail, and not to experience barriers to doing what you really want.

Sadly, many of us have a low percentage of our lives where we feel safe to be authentic without reprisal, this is because crafting a space to be authentic takes intention and effort. The best place to begin is knowing yourself. I've found that taking small steps gives me the confidence to take larger ones over time.

When we bought our house the first thing I wanted to do was paint the walls, after years of apartment living I was tired of white walls. I had always wanted a red dining room and as soon as I could I repainted our dining room. A few people told me they thought it was a bad idea, that it would be hard to paint over or that it would be too dark. I stuck by my guns, because it was something I really wanted. The results were spectacular and it is still red. People often say that it is a bold choice or that it took courage but most people say that they love it. This small step was a journey into authenticity and I still feel a sense of satisfaction about making a bold choice.

Although I have acquired some balance on this subject I still find it difficult to break even the smallest rule like having my bumper extend into the red when parking on a curb.

Today I recognize my discomfort and try to talk myself through it. I understand that following the rules is not a way to acquire love. I also understand that I can give up my superstitious tendency to follow the rules. I can be a part of society; I can treat others with respect and kindness without having to do it perfectly. Life might not involve being bad, it might involve just not being *good*. History is full of people like, Mahatma Ghandi, Georgia O'Keefe, Pancho Barnes, Josephine Baker, Henry Thoreau, Jerry Garcia, Isadora Duncan, Gertrude Stein, Bruce Springsteen, Che Guevara, Cesar Chavez, Martin Luther King who decided not to be good and go along with the rules. I aspire to be like these people who made being authentic more important than being good.

Ask for the Bag

Some years ago, my friend Alex had a dream about being trapped in an airplane that was filling with poisonous air. One of the other passengers figured out that you could survive by breathing into a bag. Alex busily set about helping to give other passengers a bag to save their lives, all the while worrying about dying from the poisonous air. I asked, "Why didn't you ask for a bag?" Alex paused and thought about it for a moment and said, "I really don't know. I should've asked for the bag." This soon became a slogan that we used for each other when we were struggling with something. One of us would say "ASK FOR THE BAG!" as a way of inspiring the other person to ask for help.

I've mentioned that one acronym for shame is <u>S</u>hould <u>H</u>ave <u>A</u>lready <u>M</u>astered <u>E</u>verything. This is the troubling idea that many of us have that we should know how to do things regardless of whether or not it is logical. This is closely tied to perfectionism in that it raises the bar of expectation to unrealistic heights. Put me in the cockpit of fighter jet and I would be ashamed that I didn't know how to fly it. It is a strange turn of my mind that I both expect to be able to do things and that I am ashamed that I can't. Imbedded in this is a peculiar kind of pride that we can or should be able to do everything.

One of the best ways to combat this thinking is to begin to assess what we genuinely can't do and to ask for help. We do this naturally with certain things, we all know we aren't brain surgeons or car mechanics so we happily pay for these services. When it comes to less obvious things like how to cope with a noisy neighbor, fire an employee or eat healthfully we sometimes expect too much from ourselves. If we haven't done it before why should we know how to do it now?

For me one of the most vital changes in my life was learning to ask for help. This is the power of counseling, group therapy and programs like Alcoholics Anonymous. People begin to experience getting help from others. They also learn how to ask for help.

I have found it particularly useful to seek out people that have experience with the challenges I am encountering. If I feel frustrated about not knowing how to refinance my home, it helps me to talk to someone who has already done it. I can apply this same logic to almost any challenge in life. I've learned to ask for help because I don't know everything. I have even acquired the habit of asking friends to help me find someone who can help. "Do you know anyone who _____?" Fill in the blank with the things that are troubling you: Quit a job they hated? Had a difficult first trimester? Was audited by the IRS?

My husband and I were trying to decide if we

should sell a rental property. In the months that preceded the sale I worried incessantly as the market plummeted and then our renters gave notice. I didn't know if it was the right time to sell or get new renters. I spent many sleepless nights combing through the alternatives. One day, I was talking to a friend who worked in real estate. It occurred to me to ask for help. I explained the situation in detail and then asked her what to do. In about 5 minutes she outlined all of our options, explained the ramifications of each one and told me what she thought was the best approach. She even offered to look at the property and help us find an agent in that area. I was flooded with a sense of relief. A decision which I was ill-equipped to make suddenly seemed simple. I was able to benefit from her expertise.

American culture doesn't particularly support this approach. Most of us are socialized to take care of ourselves. We are taught at a young age to figure out how to solve problems on our own. We glorify the individual and their achievements.

Take a moment to consider how we talk about history, Christopher Columbus who discovered the Americas, Abraham Lincoln who emancipated the slaves or Henry Ford who mass produced automobiles. If you look at our movies entire franchises are built on a single hero like John McClane in the Die Hard series or Harry Callahan as Dirty Harry or Arnold Schwarzenegger as the Terminator. The truth is that no one operates in a vacuum, we are all part of a society which is a complex fabric of people and events. Our focus on the importance of the individual is just plain wrong. Thomas Edison, famous for the invention of the light bulb and motion picture camera was in fact an aggregator of ideas. His "inventions" were actually the product of a powerful collective of great minds working together. The more accurate way to tell these stories would be, Christopher Columbus *and his crew*, Abraham Lincoln *and his cabinet*, Henry Ford *and his engineers* accomplished these astonishing feats.

We resist asking for help because it makes us feel weak or incompetent. One way to adjust our view is to consider some of the great human achievements. We all know that Neil Armstrong didn't go to space by himself. The Genome Project was the result of the work of hundreds of scientists, and the internet required millions of individuals to develop it. Recognizing that with help we can accomplish more, is one way to begin to diffuse the <u>S</u>hould <u>H</u>ave <u>A</u>lready <u>M</u>astered <u>E</u>verything kind of shame.

Begin by asking for help in simple, non-threatening ways. Try asking where to find something in the grocery store or for directions to an unfamiliar conference room. One of the surprising things you'll discover is how pleased people are to help you. When I'm shopping at the store, I'll ask if there is a good place to eat lunch in the area. What I have found is that people like sharing their knowledge and they often help me to discover hidden treasures. In an age when we have all the knowledge of the world at our finger tips, this simple means of establishing human contact can be very powerful.

Asking for help with personal and emotional issues is more challenging. It begins with developing a trustworthy network of friends. A friend taught me the very valuable principle of "Go to the love." When I was struggling with some difficult problems in my life she suggested that I seek help only from people that made me feel loved. Once I turned my attention to nurturing relationships, I found that I had been maintaining a number of unhealthy, toxic relationships. In many cases the relationships I dedicated the most attention to were the ones I feared losing. In almost every one there was a sense of imbalance in which I felt like 'less than' or that I had to prove myself to remain friends. Going toward the love meant leaving many of these relationships behind. Over time I started to notice that certain friends made me feel bad because they were mean, sarcastic or self-centered. I stopped spending time with friends who only talked about themselves or criticized others. In the course of a few years I found myself surrounded by gentler more loving people. I also found it easier to express my vulnerability and eventually to ask for help.

Early in this process, I picked one girlfriend to be a person I could learn to trust. She and I frequently talked about situations at work and in our marriages that baffled us. She would habitually say, "Can you ask for help?" when I was struggling. Almost every time she asked this question I realized that I did know someone who could help me. In almost every case when I asked someone about their experience they were able to provide some helpful advice and helped solved the problem.

If you have difficulty asking for help take a few minutes to write about your feelings. I prefer writing long hand as opposed to typing on the computer. I find that it uncovers some deeper feelings that might not otherwise emerge. Here are a few questions answer:

1. *Why am I afraid to ask for help?*

2. *Have I ever asked for help and had a positive experience?*

3. *What do I need to change in order to be able to ask for help?*

4. *Who do I trust to ask for help?*

If you are unable to answer number 4 or if the list is very short, start working on creating a larger network. Asking for help and being criticized or denied won't help you build this skill. When you begin to ask for help start with small issues that aren't packed with emotion. Can you suggest a book for me to read on vacation? Where do you like to shop for clothes? Do you have some easy recipes for party snacks? These kinds of questions are a way to test how willing someone is to help you. It will also build your confidence in asking for help on bigger issues.

Asking for help at work can be trickier since co-workers may have differing agendas and loyalties. Generally, I try to find help from a neutral party before I seek out the advice of someone close to my situation. For this reason, I have tried to foster relationships with industry peers and people who work at the same company in different departments.

The most extraordinary discovery about asking for help was that it didn't make me weak. It made me stronger. Asking for help is a natural multiplier. It increased my skill level, enhanced my innate intelligence and improved my ability to cope with difficult situations. This wasn't something that changed overnight. It took a long time before it became a habit, but it has been a worthwhile journey. I don't face situations with the same level of fear and shame. I realize that there are lots of things I don't know how to do, but that there is someone out there who does.

Perhaps the most famous and universal prayer for all of humanity is "Help!" There are situations we encounter in life that feel too big. These kinds of situations can rob us of our peace and happiness in our daily lives. I maintain what I call a 'God Can' which is like a big tin piggy bank. When I encounter a really big seemingly insoluble problem, I write it on a slip of paper and drop it in the God Can. I find that this simple act helps me let go of things I don't have the ability or resources to solve. Periodically, I empty the God Can and burn the contents. I'm almost always pleased and surprised by how many of the things I worried about are resolved. If prayer is a part of your regular spiritual practice asking God for help is another way to begin to diffuse the shame and feelings of isolation.

Boycott Apologies

At the root of shame is a sense of feeling unworthy either as a human being or in particular situation. One indicator of shame is frequent apologies. If I had counted the number of times I had apologized either in person, on the phone, or in an email it would probably be in the millions. Even with my recovery from shame I notice how often I begin correspondence with "I'm sorry..." *I'm sorry I didn't get back to you sooner. I'm sorry to bother you about this. I'm sorry but I don't agree with your conclusions.*

There is a time and a place for sincere apologies for wrong-doing, but not every day. The message "I'm sorry" implies that I have done something wrong, and most of the time when I use that phrase I haven't done anything wrong at all.

"I'm sorry" is a symptom of a larger problem. The frequent and unnecessary use of this phrase is a sign that points to a negative interior dialogue. Whenever I felt I had done something wrong, like showing up late for an event, I would immediately begin making excuses. In my head, I would think up all the possible reasons for being late and decide which was the most plausible. What I found unbearable was the idea of simply being late. I always saw any failure or flaw as proof of my belief that I wasn't enough. This drove me to make excuse after excuse and apology after apology. Some of the things I apologized for mattered, but many of them didn't. In many cases I could have let them go instead of drawing attention to my perceived shortcoming.

This problem seems to be particularly acute for women. Many of us apologize when asking for raises or for more help around the house. We often feel that attending to our needs is somehow selfish and that we need to apologize for it. Admittedly, girls are socialized from a young age to cooperate and collaborate, but this shouldn't mean that we need diminish ourselves to do so. Apologies can act as a way to smooth over a conversation or to express guilt, both real and imagined.

The problem for many women is that it becomes a kind of verbal tick that automatically reduces their personal self-worth. Men apologize much less frequently than women because they have a higher threshold for what they consider offensive[24]. In my opinion, they also realize that an apology will diminish their power in a given situation. In my experience, most men would rather move beyond the apology to fixing the situation.

---

[24] Schumann, Karina, and Michael Ross. "When Do You Owe an Apology? Depends on Gender." Association for Psychological Science, Nov. 2010,

There are a number of ways to cope with the unnecessary apology, beginning with the recognition of the habit. Try to catch yourself making unneeded apologies. Notice when you begin a sentence with "I'm sorry". You may be surprised to discover how often you write or say this phrase. See if you can reword your communication without using the word "sorry." It is incredibly empowering to discover that you can simply say what you think without excusing who you are.

A close cousin to the unnecessary apology is the diminishing adverb or clause. These are words like "just" "only" or "kind of" that lessen the impact of what you are saying. "I just wanted to let you know..." or "I kind of think we should..." Notice how this phrase has embedded in it a sense that you are an interruption or inconvenience. In an effort to sound friendly we also express a feeling of unworthiness. There are occasions where this communication would be completely appropriate, but try to notice if your language is coming from a place of feeling unworthy, mistaken or defensive. All of these may be pointing to the presence of shame.

I have learned to substitute my apologies for other more productive phrases. Instead of apologizing I try to include a positive, personal message like "I hope you are well" or "I was pleased to get your email/text/call." These phrases can serve the same purpose as the unnecessary apology without reducing your personal value.

Another good technique is to move beyond the apology to fixing the problem. If I feel I have done something wrong, is it possible to correct it? If I am late I can try not to be disruptive when I arrive. If I haven't completed a project, I can finish it. The fact of the matter is that when there is real harm done most people would prefer a correction to an apology. More often than not you will find that there is no problem to be fixed and therefore no apology required.

I'm not saying to boycott all apologies. If you have sincerely done something wrong, you should apologize. Apologies shouldn't be every day events. They should be occasional. If you find yourself crafting apologies every day you should consider working on changing your behavior. If you lie frequently, and it is causing people harm, work on telling the truth instead of apologizing all the time. There is a proper way to apologize that should, instead of causing more shame, heal the wound your actions have caused.

These are the components of a good apology:

1. *State what you have done clearly and without excuse. A good apology will never include the words "but you..." For example: "I have caused you pain by saying something which wasn't true."*

2. *State your part of the wrongdoing. Do*

*not explain the extenuating circumstances
or justify your actions. This part of the
apology should be brief and concise. For
example: "I lied"*

3. *Explain how you plan to make
   reparations for what you have done. If
   you are repaying a debt or replacing
   something broken this is the time. For
   example: "I am going to tell the other
   people involved that what I said wasn't
   true."*

4. *State your intention not to engage in this
   kind of behavior again. Then, try not do
   it again. If you do, make another apology
   and try again. Nobody is perfect.
   (Seriously, **nobody** is perfect.)*

What is important about a clean apology is that
you should be able to fill in all the blanks. If you
can't identify the harm you have done or your
role in it than an apology probably isn't
necessary. I have found that making reparations
and promising to try not to do it again are helpful
in diffusing recurring feelings of shame and guilt
over past incidents.

I recommend finding someone you trust and
talking your apology over with them before you
speak to the person you harmed. It will help you
to be clear and sometimes prevent creating a
drama where one doesn't exist. As a final note,
you should never make an apology that will

create further harm. If you cheated with your married co-worker, and his wife doesn't know, apologizing to her will only cause additional pain.

I have found tremendous relief in learning to make a proper apology and from dropping the litany of unnecessary apologies. Whether an apology is needed or not you should strive to remove this troublesome phrase from your vocabulary. In short, don't behave in ways that cause you to need to make apologies and don't apologize when you haven't done anything wrong.

Ignore that Life Behind the Curtain

Most of my life I've felt like a set dresser who arranged the movie set of my life for some outside audience. I did all the things you are supposed to do, graduated from high school, went to college, bought a car, got married. Each of these milestones was accompanied by a creeping sense that I wasn't really doing it right. I wasn't doing it the way other people were. I felt like a fake. I was terrified that someone would come "backstage" and discover what my life was really like.

I seldom expressed this feeling of being an imposter. I don't think I could even have articulated it, but I went around all the time feeling I would be caught. Someone would figure out that I didn't really know how to do whatever I was doing. Confiding in someone would only serve to uncover the secrets I had spent a lifetime protecting.

I'm naturally outgoing and social. I made friends easily and enjoyed going to parties or social events, but I always withheld a part of myself. It was as if I set up a life where I allowed people in, but all the while I lived in a secret backstage hoping no one would discover the truth about me. This contributed to a lifelong habit of keeping my weaknesses, failures and fears secret. I habitually hid the parts of myself that I thought could be used to someone else's advantage. As a result, I presented a hardened, invulnerable side to the world. When I entered any situation I always came on strong because I feared the possibility of what would happen if you knew the truth. Worse still I believed everyone else did the same thing.

I became particularly mistrustful of women. I had always been competitive and whether it was accurate or not, I felt that I was in competition with most women. The situation was particularly acute in work environments where women often were pitted against one another. Over the years I became one those girls who had many male friends. I was more comfortable with men partly because they didn't ask probing emotional questions, but also because they tended not to repeat things I told them. I had several occasions in my early years in which I felt betrayed by a girl who repeated one of my secrets. I frequently said jokingly that if I had to choose between 25 women at a baby shower or 100 drunk men in a bar I'd choose the drunk men. The bar was an environment where I understood the rules, the environment at a baby shower was completely mysterious to me.

In trying to heal my relationship with women I made a conscious decision to build a healthy friendship with another woman. I chose a friend who seemed to have similar experiences to me. I listened to her talk about other people and noticed how circumspect she was about information she had about others. In her work, she had occasion to work with famous people and I noticed she never told any stories about them. It was a sign to me that she would protect my secrets. I remember very clearly making a conscious decision to share a small secret with her. It was something I hadn't told anyone before, but it was also something I wouldn't be devastated by its disclosure. I was amazed when I told her about this terrible fear and she said 'Oh I have that too; I know exactly how you feel.' It's hard to express the sense of relief I felt knowing that I wasn't alone. Over time we built a gradual intimacy in which I felt safe sharing my anxieties, fears and failures. I think it was extremely important that she responded by sharing her secrets equally. It wasn't just that she was trustworthy, it was also her willingness to make herself vulnerable. It was a new experience for me to stop editing what I said and hiding what I considered to be the unattractive parts of myself.

One of the big mistakes I had made in the past was trusting people who were not trustworthy. As a result of both maturing, and the encouragement of others, I got better at choosing people to confide in. I began by listening to what people said when I talked them. If they talked a lot, gossiped or divulged the secrets of others it was a clue not to share my inner realm with them.

I also learned to observe if a balance existed between us. I tried to notice if the other person seemed as invested in our relationship as I was. If I was the one who did all the talking or made all the invitations I didn't pursue the relationship. Imbalanced friendships in the past left me feeling like "less than" the other person. I don't want to someone's sidekick when I was looking for genuine companionship. Choosing better friendships for better reasons has helped me move beyond perfectionism and shame.

I had been seeing a therapist regularly. She had given me a number of exercises to help me uncover some of my hidden motives and feelings. From very early on she encouraged me to make a list of my resentments and fears and to read them to her. I resisted this for a long time because she was asking me to uncover the secrets I had spent a lifetime hiding. Writing it down on paper and reading it to someone was exactly what I didn't want to do. Over a period of years, she persuaded me that I was suffering from profound feelings of shame and that I would be relieved of those feelings by saying them out loud.

It would be impossible to exaggerate the sense of relief and healing I received as a result of sharing this list with another person. At the very heart of shame is a fear of not belonging and deep sense that what is inside is so profoundly flawed. To my shock, reading a list of all my secret fears and resentments did the opposite of what I expected, it made me feel like part of society. It freed me from feeling like I was an outsider. When I finished the sharing the catalog of all my fears, resentments and failings I was greeted with the simple realization that I'm human.

Because I am stubborn, I still withheld one more secret. The black, dark, hideous truth that I felt defined who I really was. An incident in my childhood that I had never repeated to anyone. After another year, I finally admitted to my therapist that I had withheld a secret that I still couldn't tell. She suggested that I consider telling her the big black secret on my next visit. The next visit, with a knot in my stomach, I repeated this ugly incident that was, perhaps, at the core of my feelings of shame. When I was finished, my therapist sat silent for a moment, as if waiting for more. At last she said, "Is that it? That's the whole thing?" I said that it was. She said, "Well, that's a perfectly normal phase in human development. Almost every human being on earth has done that." I was shocked to the point of being speechless. For thirty years, I had cloaked my secret for fear of being ejected from human society when in fact my secret is what made me human. Instead of being an outlier, I was smack dab in the middle of the bell curve. The most important thing about this lesson is that I hadn't known I was normal because I had kept a secret. The sickness *was* the secret. A motto I often use is "I am as sick as my secrets."

Sharing secrets should be done with considerable discretion. The reason we keep secrets is because they can be harmful. I have a few principles I use in sharing my secrets. I try not to let my secrets hang around for too long, like cheese they seem to get smellier with age. I only share secrets with someone I know to be trustworthy. I don't share them with multiple people and don't share them repeatedly. I also try to avoid sharing secrets with people who are likely to give me advice. This isn't the point. I don't need to be fixed. I need to be honest. The purpose of sharing my secret is to diffuse the power it gains by being sheltered in the dark. Finally, I don't share other people's secrets. If someone tells me a secret I don't repeat it. I feel strongly that if I want other people to be trustworthy I must be trustworthy.

An unexpected consequence of giving up my secrets was I began to have better relations with other women. I realized that much of the harm of my early relationships was self-inflicted. I trusted girls who were not trustworthy. I shared inappropriately and at the wrong time. I have many women I trust now, but I chose them carefully and allowed the intimacy to grow slowly and naturally.

There is an unhealthy form of telling secrets which involves telling the truth to the wrong people. These are people who may wish to harm you or who are prone to gossip. You may also tell secrets to people who won't understand them or your reasons for sharing. Be sure that you know the person that you tell your secret to well.

You also need to consider the context of your secret. It is rarely advisable to tell your secret to someone involved in the situation. Sharing something you did that was dishonest at work with a co-worker may not be wise. I try to share my secrets with someone who is a neutral party and has nothing at stake in knowing my secret. Try to be sensitive to the person you are sharing your secret with, it may be too much for them to carry.

I made a mistake many years ago and confided something to my sister that I didn't want the rest of the family to know. For years, she had to carry that knowledge without ever telling another family member. I realize now that it was a mistake to put her into a situation of having to keep my secret.

It is also extremely important not share secrets that will harm others such as divulging a crime or an affair. It is unkind and insensitive to unburden yourself at the expense of others. If necessary, you may want to write out your secret, read it aloud privately and burn it on your own so as not to cause others harm. These sensitive secrets can also be told to therapists, priests and other clerics who take oaths of confidentiality.

There is no need to manufacture secrets or inflate old incidents so you have secrets to tell.

Your secrets may be small and seemingly unimportant or they may be large and painful. In either case, spend some time considering if these secrets are poisoning you by holding them in.

You don't have to live with secrets. Allow yourself to be free of the burden of feeling like a fake or not being a part of society because of your secrets.

No Internal Reference Point

I took up Kyudo, a form of Zen archery, as an additional meditative practice. I found a sense of peace and personal purification in the process. Initially, I thought of it as a sport, but as time went on I began to realize that the real training was happening in my mind and heart. I had the privilege of studying under Shibata Sensei XX who was the bow maker to the Emperor of Japan. His lessons have been profound and life changing on almost every level. His style was simple and concise. I believe most of his lessons were intended for individual students. I've also found that he could use the same words with two different students and it would mean two different things. This particular lesson has been so valuable I'm sharing it in the hope it will be beneficial to you.

When we shoot we stand in a line of six to eight students at time. Part of the practice is maintaining a rhythm that is consistent with the rest of the people who are shooting. One day, as I shot with the rest of the class, Sensei called out

"No internal reference point[25]" directly at me. I really had no idea what he meant. His direction prior to this had been mostly focused on my posture which I struggled with constantly. Looking at pictures and video of myself shooting I could always see the visual expression of my mental state, head hanging low, shoulders slumped, expressing a continual feeling of shame, of being unworthy or too big for the environment around me. I attempted to ask Sensei what he meant, but he didn't provide any further illumination.

For months after this lesson I contemplated 'no internal reference point'. In a literal sense, I understood that when I was shooting I tended to take clues from the other students. I was looking outside of myself to determine how I should be shooting. I recognized that I lacked the artistry and innate sense of dignity of long time students. Essentially, he was saying to me, "You need to learn to trust your natural wisdom."

Gradually, I started to notice a symptom in my life that matched my experience on the platform. Everywhere I watched for clues on how to

---

[25] Shibata Sensei XX alternated between giving instruction in Japanese and English. Instructions were sometimes translated for English speakers so it is difficult to know his exact words many years later. What I am certain of is the intent behind his words. What is often called a 'mind transmission' in Buddhism is the way many students experience teachings from a teacher of the caliber of Shibata Sensei XX.

behave. I didn't speak up in a meeting at work until someone else did. I waited for others to buy the latest style or gadget before I would buy it. I needed validation to believe that my choice was right. I asked my husband what movie we should see or where to go to dinner. It wasn't that I didn't have an opinion, it was that I didn't trust my opinion. I had "no internal reference point." I needed a second opinion to know if I was right. This was another expression of the shame in my life, just as slouching posture on the shooting platform expressed my poor self-image. Sensei's message was that I needed to find the courage to be myself *inside of myself.*

I began to see the ways in which I sabotaged myself by not listening to myself. If I knew what I wanted or how I felt, why couldn't I say it? The irony is that I expressed opinions frequently but never the ones that mattered. In fact, I often gave people unsolicited advice on all kinds of subjects. This was a defense mechanism, a way of deflecting my discomfort with myself.

Trusting Intuition

Disregarding my intuition was one of the ways I had no internal reference point. For me intuition is that small voice that makes soft-spoken suggestions or warns me that something is wrong. I used to recognize this presence of this voice and made a habit of not listening to it.

I was working on a very visible project for a new

supervisor. As a part of my job I was partnered with a retired Naval Captain who I knew was both more intelligent and more politically astute than I was. As the project progressed I saw some red flags and that small voice told first to slow down and then to stop the progress of the project. It seemed counter-intuitive at the time. I consulted with my partner and he quickly alleviated my hesitation, but the intuitive voice didn't stop. I didn't listen because I trusted him more than I trusted myself. My head just kept disregarding what my body was saying. After all, the people around me kept telling me how well things were going.

At a critical juncture in the project the whole thing came off the tracks. It was a disaster which angered my new boss and cast her in a poor light. It also seriously undercut the respect my peers had for me and my ability to lead other projects. It was one of the worst mistakes of my professional career. I believe it ultimately contributed to me leaving a job I loved. This is a classic example of no internal reference point, I placed the opinion of others above my own. I devalued my own innate wisdom because I felt that someone else was better than me. These kinds of shame-based decisions seldom turn out well.

I began to recover from my negative self-image through a combination of meditation and kyudo (Zen archery) practice. I doubt that I would have been able to think my way through this problem or solve it with conventional therapy. It wasn't a verbal or conceptual problem. Seeing my mind and my emotional state through these practices and other modes of self-discovery helped me to overcome this destructive habit.

Like many other habits I tried to break, I did make some conscious changes. I tried to speak up for myself in safe relationships. I began with small things that didn't have an emotional charge. I turned down obligations to things I didn't really want to do. I told my husband that I really wanted the garage cleaned out. I tried to stop saying 'yes' when I really meant 'no'. I also tried listening to my body more. During this time a book by Dr. Reginald Ray *Touching Enlightenment*. It helped me to begin to listen more carefully to my body and what it wanted and needed. It affected what I ate and how much I slept. I discovered that I hadn't really been listening to my body at all. It also helped me to see that I was severely over committed and burned out from all the responsibilities and activities I had.

Seeking Approval

Another area where I had no internal reference point was the need for approval. Anything I did required approval or attention in order for me to feel worthy. No matter how hard I worked or what I did I needed someone with authority to recognize and acknowledge my achievement. If they didn't I was crushed. I couldn't believe that I had done well without someone telling me that I had. What was worse was my complete inability to give myself any kind of acceptance or approval. I honestly couldn't tell if I had done a job well enough. I could never feel the satisfaction of a job well done until someone told me. If I didn't get acknowledgment I assumed I was a failure. Because of my black and white thinking and perfectionism no amount of approval was ever quite enough.

During the time, I was working creating my internal reference point I worked for a supervisor who consistently overlooked my achievements. It was my bad luck that on the delivery of some of the major accomplishments she was traveling or engaged in other more important projects. Time and again she would publically acknowledge others and (in my mind) forget about me. In a staff meeting she identified everyone that had worked on a highly visible project except me. I was so crushed I could hardly stop myself from crying. On reflection, I suspect it was an oversight, but I cried repeatedly when I thought that she didn't even know what I had done. Shortly after this disappointment I had a realization that I was causing my own pain. If I had been able to give myself the approval and recognition I desired, I wouldn't need others to do it for me. If I had had an internal reference point I wouldn't need an external one.

The Good Girl (Really, Again?)

Another place that my lack of internal reference point showed up was in my proclivity to follow rules. I had hardly ever done a single bad thing in my life. I had to go back to my teenage years to find anything that was moderately bad. I had lived most of my life on the straight and narrow, showing up for work on time, paying my taxes and playing along with what was expected of me by my parents, friends and colleagues. I seldom did anything surprising. I really felt like I was at everyone's beck and call but my own. I realized how rarely I thought about what I wanted on a deep level. I had no idea how to feel satisfied. This became my new objective, to understand what I really wanted and how I could give myself the approval I craved. Instead of following rules and complying with others expectations I tried to see what would please me.

A Work in Progress

I knew that I wanted to be author, that I loved to paint and I wanted to be around horses. So, I took small steps to adjust my life to make these things possible. I also tried to stop dancing to other people's music. I tried to do things because I wanted to do them, not because other people wanted me to do them. In many cases, there was little change in my outward actions, but inwardly I was doing what I did for different reasons. In some cases, the people around me were frustrated that I stopped doing things I had done in the past, and I began to realize that other people's feelings were not my responsibility. Going through life marching to someone else's drum was profoundly unsatisfying.

If others didn't like what I was doing I realized that they had a problem that I couldn't solve. I was profoundly uncomfortable at first. I felt like I was doing something bad and being selfish. I also felt that I was shirking my responsibilities simply because I had agreed to do them in the past. This sense of hyper-responsibility was part of my shame-based thinking. I felt that in order to belong in society I had to *do* things. If I didn't do what people wanted than I wasn't worthwhile. I know now that I don't have to do something simply because it needs to be done. My habit of raising my hand because no one else did needed to stop because it was based on seeking outside approval and feeling responsible of the emotional state of others.

Change involved spending more time on my own. I am, by nature, extroverted and spent most of my free time doing something with friends or family. I began to allow myself to sit quietly alone, to listen to my own mind and not fear silence. I turned off my radio in the car and I went on solitary meditation retreats. I began to get to know who I am instead of focusing on what I do. I found that I am both tougher and more vulnerable than I thought. I have developed a sense of appreciation for who I am.

I've also accepted the fact that I'm profoundly ordinary. The things I say, and do, what I fear, is pretty much what most human beings experience. I realized that I could relax and enjoy the ride more, and stop driving myself to be the hero of the incredible drama I had been writing in my head. In school, I had often said I didn't fear getting an F, I feared getting a C. I feared being average and now I began to realize that ordinary people do extraordinary things, but on some level, we are all ordinary. Most important was the recognition that this is completely fine.

Another important aspect of developing an internal reference point is realizing that many things I consider mandatory aren't. For years, I turned up at social events because I felt that I had to. Self-examination led me to the realization that my presence isn't that important. If I don't show up for my husband's co-worker's birthday party or the latest business networking event, I'm not likely to be missed. The discovery that I can spend my time the way I want to has been revolutionary.

This is not an excuse to be selfish. There are still things I have to do that I don't want to do, but I've found that when I make decisions for affirmative reasons, instead of negative ones the experience is much more satisfying. I might go to my husband's co-worker's birthday party after all but I'll go because my husband doesn't want to go by himself or because I like the people he works with not because I have to.

Making decisions in this way leads to a feeling of directing my life instead of drifting along and responding to the wishes of others. It requires more thought and it requires knowing my own mind. One useful way to begin to make these decisions is by thinking about how you want to feel. When I place the desired result at the front of my decision-making I begin to get tremendous clarity[26].

Ultimately my journey toward having an internal reference point has been a long one. I'll probably need to be conscious of it for the rest of my life. Meditation[27] has been an excellent way to get in touch with my own mind.

Try mapping out a week in your life. I do this hour by hour for all of my waking hours. I color code activities by the type of activity. For example; blue is work, yellow is household responsibilities, green is self-care. Once you do this look at the colors in your week. If you work 40 hours, the first thing you'll notice is how much of your week goes to work. An examination of the colors may reveal imbalances.

---

[26] Danielle LaPorte has created an excellent tool called The Desire Map to help you understand how to create the life you really want. I highly recommend it.

[27] See the chapter Taming that Bitch in Your Head for more detail on meditation. There is also recommended reading in the back of the book.

Continue looking at your calendar and ask yourself the following questions:

Does my week look balanced? Is there too much of any one color?

Which of these things do I feel I have to do? Is it true that I have to do them?

How do I feel when I'm doing these things? Is this how I want to feel?

Are there any activities I can or should say no to?

Which of these things make me feel good? Is there any way to increase those things?

I've found this system of color coding gives me clarity on where my time is being spent. You don't need to turn your life upside down, simply try to recognize the things that you're doing as a result of external pressure. Maybe it's fine to vacuum every other week, maybe you can buy cupcakes for the school bake sale instead of making them from scratch, maybe you should go to yoga instead of the baby shower for the neighbor you barely know.

I also highly recommend any kind of practice or healing that helps you connect with your body. Your body is a potent source of wisdom. It has a deep non-conceptual knowing that is *the* internal reference point Sensei encouraged me to seek. For me a mixture of meditation, Kyudo, yoga,

Pilates, stretching, Shen therapy, massage therapy, Reiki therapy and Qi Gong has helped create this connection. There are innumerable other modes of exercise and healing you can try. The main thing is to be gentle with yourself and to listen. You have powerful, secret wisdom within you waiting to be heard.

Not Picking and Choosing

The human mind is a powerful tool. Most of us use it daily and barely notice the ways we use it. It guides the simplest motor skills and shapes the way we view the world around us. Most of the time we don't think about how it does what it does. Consider for a moment the rush of information that you receive every second. All five of your senses are sampling the environment and quickly organizing the stimuli to make sense out of them. Most of this is invisible until our brain sends out a warning message like "Smoke!" which causes us to investigate if there is a threat. Most of the time this behind-the-scenes organization is useful to us but it can get in the way of our quality of life.

Picking and choosing is a normal daily activity. You like to sleep in or get up early. You prefer cereal or you dislike cold breakfasts. You like showers more than baths. All day long we are confronted with a barrage of *this* or *that*. We engage in continual dialogue of wanting, rejecting or ignoring whatever situation we find ourselves in. It is a human tendency to prefer pleasure over pain. For many of us our pursuit of what is pleasurable and our rejection of what is painful can become pathological to the degree that we self-medicate at the first sign of discomfort.

The concept of equanimity seems completely contrary to this natural function of the human brain. According to the Merriam-Webster Dictionary the word equanimity comes from the Latin word *aequanimitas* which is a combination of "aequus" ("even") and "animus" ("soul" or "mind"), taken together they mean "with even mind." It is often defined as composure, calmness, or cool-headedness. All of which sound like desirable traits but aren't so easy to achieve. In the Buddhist tradition equanimity is often likened to maintaining your seat in the saddle on horseback. I like the image of not being buffeted, or falling off if your horse changes gait or stumbles. Something wonderful happens, keep your seat. Something terrible happens, keep your seat. Nothing happens, keep your seat.

For years, I suffered from terrible migraines. I tried medication and multiple home remedies and never really found anything that would lessen the intense pain. Most of the time I would retire to a dark room and try to sleep if I could. With my new meditation practice I decided not to avoid my migraine and try exploring the sensory experience. Instead of pushing away the excruciating pain I decided to accept it and examine it. What I expected was 12 solid hours of agonizing, debilitating pain. As I lay in bed in the darkness, I brought my attention to the pain and made a surprising discovery. The pain modulated, it was sharp and acute for minutes at a time, but then it stopped. I had relaxed and my symptoms diminished. I relaxed, because I began to accept the headache as it was.

When the pain stopped, I felt a rush of euphoria and exceptional well-being until the pain started again. Until then I had never experienced the good feeling because my mind was completely fixed on the pain. This led to the realization that there are many things in life I didn't have an accurate perception of and that I had never truly experienced.

I also gradually came to understand that my feelings and experiences were not as pure as I thought they were. Joy has a slightly sad and poignant quality. Excitement is often tinged with anxiety and fear. Anger is attended by clarity and a sense of purpose. Life and its emotions are full of complex and seemingly conflicting feelings. I would not have discovered this without the insight I've gained from regular meditation.

A great deal of shame is generated by rejecting what is and longing for what is not. For years, I wanted to be a petit slender woman with straight hair. I am a tall, substantial woman with curly hair. I was unhappy with the body I had and tried to reduce it to something less. This was the genesis of my habit of starving and restricting my food. I was trying to make myself smaller. Seeing it in retrospect I realize how pointless it was, perhaps if I had embraced my size I wouldn't have suffered so much. Because of my dissatisfaction with my own lot I was consumed with envy. I always wanted to be thinner, or prettier, or smarter, or richer. This kind of grasping only led to unhappiness. The conundrum is we believe that we will be happy when get something we don't have, but in pursuit of those things we never recognize and appreciate the things we do have. I'm most acutely aware of the wasted time in my own life when I look at old pictures of myself. I see an ordinary girl traveling the world, laughing with friends, enjoying family events, advancing in her career. A girl who had every reason to be happy but who seldom was. It is the tragedy I created in my own life by picking and choosing even among things I couldn't change.

When I traveled in India it was full of difficulties, trains run late or don't come at all, water buffaloes stop traffic and the heat can be stifling. When I first arrived, I was shocked at the conditions that most Indians considered normal. How could a main street be shut down for a whole day while the local fisherman protested new government regulations? One night I was having dinner with friends when the power went off unexpectedly. I immediately jumped up to find a candle but all my Indian friends sat impassively. I asked if anyone noticed the power went off.

One friend replied, "Yes, it will come back on."

"When?" I asked anxiously.

"When it comes on." As someone accustomed to living in a society where water and electricity were as dependable as the sunrise, I was barely able to comprehend their apparent lack of concern with not having power. I soon learned that this was the key to living in India, accepting things as they are. The most surprising thing about most Indians is their vitality, their seemingly unquenchable joy in living. I think this level of acceptance, known as equanimity, in some spiritual traditions, is the key to living with a sense of well-being. Like my Indian friends I began to realize that I only hurt myself by resisting what is.

If you begin to think about this principle you are likely to realize that many of the events in your life are colored by your reaction. Your reaction is generated by your judgment. A friend of mine had her garage catch on fire and lost many of her personal mementos. When I commented that it was disaster she said "One fire is about equal to moving three times." She decided she would have cleaned her garage and gotten rid of all those things eventually, the fire just caused it to happen faster. She chose not see the fire as good or bad, instead of being devastated she accepted the situation as it was.

In Western culture, we often use our beliefs to bring us to a place of equanimity. We say that God will never give us more than we can handle or that what doesn't kill us makes us stronger. This is an artificial way to achieve equanimity, we remove the judgment by believing the outcome will be good. Developing a quality of equanimity goes one step beyond that by detaching from the judgment of good and bad. Things simply are as they are. "God causes the rain to fall on the good and evil[28]." The principle of equanimity suggests the rain is neither good nor bad. You aren't being tested or judged, you are simply experiencing water falling from the sky, which is different than when the sun is out.

A friend some years ago taught me the very useful phrase which I use on an almost daily basis "Pause when agitated or doubtful." Many of us are raised to respond to discomfort with action. You mind screams, "If you don't like it DO SOMETHING!" The idea of sitting still with discomfort is unfamiliar to most of us. It was for me until I began to implement this principle. The whole source of our discomfort often unfolds in less than a second. Someone says or does something that angers us, frightens us or confuses us. We judge it as "bad", and then launch into our plan for response. It happens so quickly we hardly even notice. What we often do notice is that we are agitated or doubtful. These two valuable feelings can signal that something isn't right. Instead of responding with our ordinary lightning quick judgment and reaction

---

[28] Matthew 5:45

we can pause, notice our feelings, and even lean into them.

Once I started doing this I noticed that my feeling of urgency was either inaccurate or in some cases almost pathological. It turns out there are precious few things in life we need to respond to immediately. If the driver in the car in front of you slams on their brakes, that requires immediate attention. Otherwise, the phone calls or emails, requests for your attention, seeming crises and demands for immediate action can mostly wait. Take five minutes or even a whole day to assess how you feel and how you want to respond or if you want to respond at all.

It would be impossible to count the number of arguments I have averted, bad decisions I delayed or simple misunderstandings I have avoided in the past decade as result of this simple principle of pausing. It has become habitual for me to pause for even a split second, especially in emotionally charged situations. This helps to uncover the ways in which I am resisting some things and clutching at others. Agitation, anxiety or impatience can be a signal that I have a strong attachment or revulsion for a particular situation or person.

Try pausing and see if you can catch yourself and if your story line is contributing to the pain you feel. You can recognize the ways in which picking and choosing are forcing you to act when possibly no action is required. Picking and choosing can be a very dangerous enemy. It can feed our victim mentality and trap us into making the same mistake over and over. *This is bad. Why does this always happen to me? Why can't I ever catch a break? I hate it when this happens.* Soon we spiral down into a familiar cycle of frustration, victimization and ultimately shame. It all began with the idea that what is happening is a bad thing. Not judging the situation can short circuit the whole pattern and leave you feeling empowered instead.

Many of us obsess over making the wrong decision or not knowing what to do. This is also the trap laid by picking and choosing. What if all decisions are equal? What if taking a new job or staying where you were both equally good decisions? What if it didn't make any difference which pre-school your daughter got into? What if moving to be closer to your family or relocating to Japan are equally good decisions? What if there is no right answer? You can feel the freedom of knowing you aren't doing something wrong. You are just taking the next action that makes the most sense to you. If it doesn't work out, you can make a different decision and that won't be wrong either. It's the judgment we place on ourselves. The story line we attach that says we *can* take a wrong turn. We tell ourselves that we can marry the wrong person, take the wrong job, buy the wrong house but what if they are all equally good or equally bad?

Nothing Happened

The decisions that we make about things being good or bad fuel the drama in our life. For many years, I was addicted to drama. If nothing was happening, I felt like I wasn't alive. In this respect, it didn't seem to matter to me if the drama was good or bad, so long as there was drama. Most of this drama was largely imaginary. When I began to understand the idea of equanimity I realized that most of the events in life aren't dramas. In fact, the vast majority of life is stunningly ordinary. Most days aren't filled with heroic narrative dramas, most days nothing happens. If you examine even dramatic events in our lives, we see that often nothing actually happened to us.

Watching a brush fire consume hundreds of acres on television may be spectacular and exciting, you may even be evacuated from your home, but ultimately nothing really happens, at least not until your house burns down. It is our own minds that create a bad day or good day. It is the story line we attach to events that turn it into a drama. I have come to recognize experiencing the present moment without bias is one of the great gifts of being human. In modern society, free from the threat of being ambushed by wild beasts or starving to death, we can stroll through our days and enjoy the remarkable phenomenal world. We have the leisure to taste, smell, and feel the world at large. It turns out life without drama is far from boring, it has the power to be ineffably joyful.

When I was laid off of a job, I called a spiritual teacher and told him of my misfortune. He said enthusiastically, "Congratulations! You haven't been happy there for a long time." In my head, losing a job was always bad. His response made me re-examine my perspective. As it turned out, I spent the next year doing many things I enjoyed and taking advantage of the unexpected free time. There were many, many times that I commented on something I wouldn't have been able to do if I had been working. Instead of turning the job loss into a drama, I simply went on to the next thing in my life. Ultimately that year turned out to be the transition from an unhappy life to a much more fulfilling one.

Beginning to recognize that life and its events don't require judgment or instant reaction can lead to tremendous freedom. Recognizing that your judgments fuel your shame can help you to begin to recover from it. Much of the negative self-talk we use is caused by our self-judgment and our relentless demands for perfection. One tool I often use when something doesn't go according to plan or when I'm disappointed by an outcome is to say, "Well, glad that's over." It helps me to acknowledge my disappointment, drop my judgments and move on. The most useful tool I have found to cultivate equanimity is a regular meditation practice.

Head Where Your Feet Are

I once heard someone say that all thoughts are either reminiscing, commentary or forecasting. This relates to the idea of picking and choosing. Our mind is in a continual state of deciding what we think about any number of situations. The average human being has 20,000 to 70,000 thoughts per day. That's a veritable firehouse of information streaming through the elegant wiring of our brains. I don't know if anyone has ever done the science but based on my own experience I would say that 90% of conscious thoughts relate to worrying about the future or regretting the past. I, like most people I know, don't spend much time in the present. For me I am constantly see-sawing back and forth between guilt and judgment about something I did wrong or fear of the future. It is completely exhausting.

The idea of being in the present moment without judgment is an unfamiliar practice. Our sense of smell, sight, taste, sound and touch are all rooted in the present moment. All of our memories are simply recalling some sensual stimulus from the past. Why is it so difficult for us to *stay here in the now*? I believe one reason is the essential discomfort we have with experience we haven't labeled. Our mind is engaged full-time in sorting things into careful piles, *I like this... I hate this... I don't care about that....* Try to imagine going to a movie, eating a meal or walking through a museum without judging. It feels odd, even a little uncomfortable. The present moment without judgment can be terrifying. Without judging the present moment, we may even be paralyzed and not know what to do next. The challenge is that the human brain is not wired for living in the past or the future. It is a tool that is at its best when it interprets the present moment.

I often say that if I had a friend who consistently gave the same kind of false information as my own brain does. I'd quit listening to them. My brain has repeatedly projected entirely inaccurate futures.

There's a recession and I'm going to lose my house.

Wrong.

These people I'm working with aren't going to like me.

Wrong.

I'm never going to learn how to use this software.

Wrong.

In fact, almost none of the things I fear have happened. My projections are so consistently wrong I wonder why I listen to them at all.

In the same way, I have misrepresented my past. In high school, I struggled never entirely grasped chemistry. For years, I told myself that I had to avoid anything that involved science, until I had a job where I had to read scientific papers and analyze statistical information. It turned out it was easy for me and I had spent years believing an old story written by a student in her first chemistry class. This is the genesis of much shame-based thinking: *I didn't master something the first time I tried it so I'm a failure.* What's more, my mind has hazy and faulty perceptions of what happened. According to many recent studies memory is far from accurate. Memories are an amalgamation of the sense perceptions, the story line you attach and the subsequent events. Often our brains re-write history when it receives new information. Examine some of your older memories and notice anachronisms in them. For example, I find it almost impossible to envision my local bank in the town where I grew up without an ATM machine, yet in my childhood there were no ATMs.

I often think of the scene in the movie *A Beautiful Mind* in which the brilliant Dr. John Nash tries to think his way out of a mental problem. His wife gently tells him that his brain *is* the problem so it won't be able to fix the problem. This is the conundrum for all of humanity. Many of our problems are created by our thinking and we can't think our way out of it. Or maybe we *can.* The essential problem is not disabling or overcoming our minds, it is understanding it and harnessing its awesome capacity.

Our brain is an extremely elegant device for collecting phenomenal experience. It can collect millions of bits of data from the environment and synthesize it into meaning. The rain outside means you may need to carry an umbrella. The smell of hot coffee means that the coffee maker is brewing fresh coffee. The sound of the siren means to be alert for danger. All of this is useful. Except we find ourselves recalling a past instance where we slipped and fell in the rain, or when the coffee burnt our tongue or when we were almost hit by a fire truck and we are catapulted into the past or we fear whatever may be waiting in the future. The present moment is lost in the sea of past and future. The important point is that our recollection of the past and our projection about the future is almost *never* right.

I first began to learn to stay in the present when I learned to meditate. I was surprised to discover that in the present I wasn't worried, nervous, angry or frightened. In the present, everything was fine. All I need in the present is to deal with what is right in front of me. In the present I can appreciate the cool of the rain, drink my coffee and pull over so the fire truck can pass. Being in the present moment gives me an advantage because I won't miss important clues, like the tail lights of the car in front of me or the oil patch on the road. Opening my senses to allow the present moment in can be joyful. Most important in the present there is no opportunity for shame. I'm not judging I'm simply experiencing and if I find myself judging me I can simply return to the present moment.

This is the genesis of this very useful expression, 'head where your feet are.' Whenever I find myself in a tailspin it is almost always because my head is somewhere else. It is projecting what will happen if I'm late, or reliving an argument with my husband, none of which is happening now. *Now* is the only place I am able to find peace and happiness. *Now* is the place that my mind can relax and enjoy the stimuli it is receiving. *Now* is where I can actually taste the coffee or feel the thrill of success. It is all happening right NOW.

When my husband and I went on our honeymoon we took many pictures of beautiful beaches and golden sunsets. Looking back many years later the thing I remember most distinctly is that we woke up at sunrise one morning and took a long silent walk together. It was one of the most beautiful mornings of my life, I didn't have my camera and we weren't caught up in discursive chatter. We were jointly experiencing the moment. Some years later, I stopped taking pictures on vacation all together because I realized the experience of the moment was more profound and beautiful if I wasn't trying to record it on film. I do take pictures of beloved friends and family and enjoy seeing pictures from events I've attended, but I've found planting myself firmly in the present moment is the best way to preserve a fond memory.

For most of us staying in the present is unfamiliar. The more time I devote to meditation the easier I find it. I began with a very simple practice of bringing my attention to my breath. I breathed in, following the breath in and then breathed out. Without exception, two or three breaths will almost always bring me to the present moment.

Another wonderful tool is to scan my body for somatic feedback. I ask myself 'what am I feeling in my lower abdomen, my stomach and my chest right now?' I even try to describe the feeling. *My chest is tight. There's a knot in my throat. My jaw is clenched.* All of these things are clues to what is happening. Over the years I have developed a kind of emotional lexicon. I know when my throat feels tight that I'm feeling like a victim unable to speak up. I know that butterflies in my chest is anxiety and sometimes excitement. These somatic responses clue me in to the fact that something in my environment is affecting me.

I find that inquisitiveness is a good tool for bringing me to the present, particularly when interacting with other human beings. If I ask myself the very simple question 'What is happening here?' I often discover surprising or even delightful answers. In business meetings, I am often able to find humor instead of dread by simply tuning into the antics of each person's individual ego. Sitting in traffic I might notice the warmth of the sun on my leg, the beauty of the singer's voice on the radio or comic dance of a dog in the back seat of the car next to me. Much of the information available to my senses is lost because I don't use the present moment to really take it in.

I was responsible for picking up a well-known Lama at LAX at 5:00 PM on a Friday night. Getting on the 405 freeway on a Friday night is the single most dreaded traffic experience in the city of Los Angeles. All week long I nursed a resentment toward the person who had booked a flight that arrived at 5:00 PM and the person that asked me to pick-up the Lama and drive him across town. With the Lama in tow I got onto the freeway to be confronted by exactly what I expected, thousands of cars virtually parked on the freeway as far as the eye could see. The Lama sat quietly in back seat. After a few moments sitting in traffic he said quietly "Look at all these cars. Where do you suppose they are all going?" I thought, "Good question, where are they all going?" In a split second he moved me from suffering in my anxiety about how long we'd sit in traffic to the present. There have been a few occasions in my lifetime I have had the privilege of being in the presence of men and women who have highly developed spiritual practices; some of them have been Christian, some Jewish, some Hindu and some Buddhist. I've observed that all of them have had one thing in common, a deep sense of inquisitiveness about the present.

I've learned from moving into the present is almost always. In the onslaught of my personal storytelling about the past and the present I often miss what's *really* happening. I often rush from moment to moment and miss the wealth of what *is* happening. Training myself to stay in the moment, feel what is actually happening and experience Now has changed my world outlook. I've begun to see how each person I encounter has their own special qualities, each circumstance has its own individual taste and I appreciate the sumptuous buffet available to my senses in every moment. Now I see that every moment is precious if I'm available for it, but only if I relax in the present. The world and its inhabitants are essentially good.

This is what's meant by "head where your feet are", being willing to experience Now instead of being lost in thought in the past or the future. Bringing my attention to my lungs breathing in and out helps me to be right where my feet are. As one of my friends says, riffing on the 1971 classic book by yogi Ram Dass, "Be here Now, or get here soon."

That Time I Lived Under a Bridge with My Cat

I've always been afraid of not having money. I didn't grow up in an environment where we talked much about money, banking or investments though I do remember being aware of the idea of being in debt at an early age. I remember hearing my parents arguing about debts in hushed voices and feeling a sense of shame. I couldn't have identified it at the time but now I recognize that I was ashamed of the idea of being poor.

We weren't poor. We were just an average American family with what I suspect was an average amount of debt and an average amount of conflict around money. I can't remember a time when I wasn't worried about money. It seems as if I was always conscious of status. I noticed when other families appeared to have more money and longed to be wealthy. At the same time, I deeply resented people who I thought of as rich. Some of my peers were given cars on their 16th birthday and I felt I deserved to have a new car and should be allowed to buy anything I wanted. I genuinely believed that having more money would cure my feeling of being insufficient. In my experience, these feelings are very common in middle class

America. My belief that there wasn't enough money to go around, combined with my natural competitiveness made for an unpleasant stew of anxiety and ambition.

I had a crippling feeling of lack all the time that didn't necessarily relate to the balance in my bank account. I just felt afraid that disaster would strike at any moment. The slightest rumor of layoffs at work and I would instantly see myself as a bag lady living under a bridge. The funny thing is I worried what would happen to my cat in these circumstances and never considered that my husband was working or that my family would probably help us out before we were homeless. The main point is that my fears were unnatural and I experienced them in isolation. It was another example of the way that shame kept me from asking for help and simultaneously believing that I should already know how to master everything.

Underpinning all my anxiety and shame about money was a basic lack of clarity. When I went away to college I didn't understand how checking accounts worked and was afraid to ask. Later, I continued the same pattern when it came to credit cards, taxes, insurance and mortgages. I stumbled along crossing my fingers and hoping I wouldn't get into too much trouble. Eventually, I found myself in five figure credit card debt, underwater on a condominium and out of work with no idea how it happened.

I reached my bottom with money and tried something I had never done before. I tried getting clarity about my situation. I sat down and totaled up all my debts and figured out my monthly expenses. For the first time in my life I knew exactly how much money I needed to survive. To my complete surprise I was *relieved*. The situation was bad, but at least I was clear about *how* bad. Over the next five years my husband and I gradually worked our way out of debt. We cut up our credit cards, got an education on real estate short sales and started paying cash for everything. We also sought help from an accountant and eventually from financial planners. We attended a very helpful class[29] that taught us how to talk to each other about money in a healthy way and how to navigate in the financial world. Our lives are completely different today but I don't think I would have changed if I hadn't faced my shame related to money.

I had terrible problems with envy. I found myself comparing myself to celebrities and friends. I never quite measured up. I looked at other people's jewelry, clothing, cars and houses and always found myself lacking. Social media, magazines and television shows fueled these

---

[29] Financial Peace University is a class offered by Dave Ramsey that explains how money works and also helps you devise a plan to get out of debt. We found taking the class in-person was very helpful, it is also offered as an online streaming class.

feelings to an unhealthy degree. My haircut was never cool enough. My house was never big enough. My life was never happy enough. One simple fix for this was to stop looking at media that presented other peoples' amazing lives. I haven't opened an *In Style* magazine for about 10 years and honestly don't miss it, (well, except for the gift guide....)

I always ran around feeling that I had to exchange hours for money. This led to exhausting cycle of putting in more hours to get more money. Once I moved from hourly jobs to salaried jobs I transferred that logic to promotions. If I needed to earn more I just needed to work more. It didn't ever occur to me that my boss might see my long hours as a sign of inefficiency. The trouble with this thinking was that I only have a finite amount of time[30] and energy. As with so many flawed ideas, I couldn't see that my problem was my own thinking.

The most important work for me was inside. I struggled with feelings of lack and poverty. As I've gotten older I've come to understand that these feelings are seldom related to the facts of my life. I could feel this way even if I had a million dollars in the bank because money wasn't my problem. My thinking was my problem.

---

[30] *The Big Leap* by Gay Henrickson was a huge help with my thinking about time. I suffered from a fear of not have enough time for years.

The first thing I was willing to do was adopt this affirmation that I said aloud to myself daily for years and still repeat it regularly.

I am enough, I have enough, I do enough.

Later I started carrying a little deck of index cards with the following affirmations on them:

I am the fortunate daughter of an abundant universe.

I am queen of a lovely empire.

I have more money than I can spend.

I am whole, complete and perfect as I am.

Time is my friend and ally.

I manifest everything I need with ease and grace.

Each of these affirmations deals with a different aspect of flawed thinking about money. These affirmations began to reshape my thinking and I started to notice that I generally have what I need. This accompanied another important shift in my thinking. I always wanted to win the lottery so I could just stop thinking about money forever[31]. The trouble with this thinking is that it would fuel my tendency to be completely self-reliant. I began to understand that part of my

---

[31] An example of Silver Bullet Thinking

spiritual path was trusting that I would be taken care of no matter what. I began to understand that I have always had the money I needed *when I needed it.* It's like buying a ticket for a plane when I need to go somewhere. I don't need to stockpile boarding passes for every possible destination when I'm going to fly somewhere. I just need one boarding pass for one destination. This realization completely changed the way that I thought about wealth. Most days I believe I'll have what I need when I need it. It isn't necessary to worry about it before I need it.

These affirmations also helped me to see that I'd always believed there is a finite amount of wealth. If others had it, it precluded me having it. Now I understand there is enough if I believe there is enough. I see myself as being able to provide for myself now and in the future. This feeling of universal abundance has been very powerful in building my personal self-esteem.

I once heard that wealthy people have on average seven streams of passive income. This means finding ways to earn money with little or no effort. Part of my shift in the past few years is to move from the idea of having to exchange hours for dollars to exploring ways to generate passive income. In fact, I've made it a goal to create seven streams of passive income. This means creating products that will be purchased repeatedly, considering rental or business investments, creating new products, writing books and exploring new lending opportunities.

The main point for me has not been to become wealthy. It has been to become healthy in the way I relate to money. I budget, I keep track of what I spend and I attempt to have clarity about my financial situation. When I feel hazy or unsure I try to stop and get clarity. When I feel the old feelings of lack I pull out my affirmations or talk to a friend about how I feel. I try to avoid isolation whenever I can. Clarity has been the main cure for my feeling of shame about money. Increasing clarity has also diffused my sense of isolation and hopelessness about not having enough.

So, the cat's fine. Neither one of us has ever had to live under a bridge or go without food.

You Have to
Get on a Bus

As a child, I was fascinated with all things spiritual. I was not raised by a church-going family and I felt deprived of an important life experience. One of my great aunts sent me a small white New Testament with my name engraved on the front. This quickly became my most treasured possession. I carried it with me like a talisman when we traveled I believed that it kept us safe because God was with us. My parents were neither atheists nor agnostics; they were "a-religious." Neither of them had a particular fondness for any organized religion and offered very little in the way of religious training.

As I grew older I sampled many religious traditions and explored the realm of religion, God, and spirituality down many avenues. The one unalterable conclusion I came to again and again is that all of mankind longs for, and needs, something greater than him or herself to believe in.

For many reasons, most of which are dull and cliché, I had a period in my life which I refer to as '10 years of radio silence.' I didn't have any kind of spiritual practice or religious expression. It was during this time that I met Hannah. As a teenager, Hannah had been in a terrible accident in which she had nearly bled to death. She experienced floating above the scene of the accident and facing the decision to leave this life. I asked her what she learned from her near-death experience. She said "I learned that your spiritual life is like sitting on a bus bench waiting for a bus. Many of them come by. There is no right bus or wrong bus but you have to get on one of them. You can't just sit on the bench and never get on the bus." Hannah's message helped me to realize that I had been sitting on a bus bench for 10 years watching the buses go by. I knew it was time to get on a bus.

My spiritual life had passed through many stages I had been childish, self-sufficient, dogmatic, devout, well-trained, evangelical, monastic and lazy. Spirituality is a constantly evolving and changing path, not a fixed destination. In fact, I believe the only real enemy of true religion is a closed or fixed mind. I've come to believe that one of the keys to living successfully is the recognition that there is something greater than yourself.

Here I must give credit to Bill Wilson and the founders of AA who popularized the term 'Higher Power.' I believe that any time human beings believe they are omnipotent and the master of their environment they run amok. The simple, humble recognition that there are forces greater than any individual is not only a healthy, but also obvious. This is not a religious book and

I have no intention of endorsing any particular religion or belief. I don't wish to offer an opinion on who or what is the true higher power. For some that Higher Power might be something they call God, for others it might be Nature, or the general life force that animates the planet. Whatever it may be I believe that the humility of recognizing I am not the ultimate power on earth has helped greatly in my recovery from shame. It has made it possible for me to relax and be a part of the great dance of being human without feeling that I might take a wrong, irreparable step. It reduces the consequences of my actions and therefore lessens my feeling that I am a terrible mistake. It also frees me from the tyranny of perfectionism because I recognize that I am not a god with responsibility for every single thing that happens around me.

Not long after I heard Hannah's story a friend encouraged me to find a spiritual path that I could follow. From her experience, she said that I would be helped by belonging to a community, having a spiritual leader and following a specific path. I set out to find a spiritual path that resonated with me, this time not out of a feeling of lack, as I had done in my childhood, but out of sense of caring for myself and my well-being. For months, I asked everyone I encountered if they had a spiritual path and if they could tell me about it. I discovered practicing Jews, Buddhists, Christians, Wiccans, Pagans, Hindus, Yogis and various kinds of meditators were all around me.

Then I began reading. I would go to large bookstores and sit in the *Spirituality/Religion* aisles for hours sampling every kind of spiritual experience I could find. One of the main realizations I made during this time was the breadth and depth of human religious experience. There are hundreds of kinds of experiences and all of them seemed to sprout from the same seeds. I also saw how many claimed to be the "True Religion" disavowing other practices which taught the very same principles. It was a though all humanity was cooking with the same recipe and saying only their recipe was Momma's Real Original Sauce. I finally understood the lesson behind Hannah's bus bench. Momma gave us all the recipe but it's up to us to actually cook.

During this exploration, I tried to maintain an attitude of open mindedness. I recognized that exploration means entering the unknown. If I stuck to the traditions I already knew there was a likelihood that I might not discover a new path. I had long been a student of religion and was familiar with both the beliefs and the texts of most of the world's major religions. Intellectually I was well prepared to examine my options. At the same time, I understood that this inquiry was not an intellectual endeavor but a heart journey. So, for a few years, I sampled various paths.

I always liken this time to the trailhead I remember visiting in a national park. It is a large clearing with signs pointing in different directions

"To the Falls", "To the Valley", "To the Meadow." I wandered around considering the signs and their relative benefits but didn't really know where I wanted to go. I thought "I bet the meadow is beautiful, but I've heard that the valley is beautiful too and if I went to the falls I could take a swim." On my spiritual journey, I had deliberated at the trailhead for so long I hardly remembered that I had set out on a hike to begin with. Then one day, by pure happenstance, a book arrived in the mail. It was a small five-dollar book I had ordered to qualify for free shipping while shopping online. When I found it in the box I wondered what it was and set it aside to read later. A few months later I tossed it into my suitcase to read on weekend trip.

That weekend I had a profound and life-changing experience. I opened the book and read only a few pages. My heart leapt. I felt as if the author were speaking directly to me. I knew for certain that this was the path that I had been searching for. I knew with my heart, not my head, that I could start up this trail and I would be happy with the destination. I stopped deliberating and immediately searched out the spiritual community described in the book. I attended classes and quickly read the book cover to cover. Twelve years later I am still certain that I am on the right path for me.

One of the most important elements about my personal search for a spiritual path was sincerity.

I genuinely wanted to find a real practice that would work for me. For me it was crucial to be open-minded and not eliminate any options based on my personal biases or fears. During the early investigation, *nothing* was off the table. I found that things that had never appealed to me still didn't. But, I did discover new paths which I investigated. For example, I had very little interest in becoming a Pagan, but Pagan writing did lead me to the realization that many traditions exclude the feminine and disregard the power of nature, something which did appeal to me. Another critical part of my journey was diligence. I worked hard at finding a spiritual path and it took time, I didn't expect it to come to my front door and knock, though ultimately it did[32]. I believe it came to me because I was earnestly pursuing all avenues. I listened to my heart through this process. If I went to a service or listened to a talk from a teacher or leader and I didn't feel excited, happy or energized I didn't force myself to like it. I just moved on, trusting my own innate wisdom.

Finally, I did make a choice. I didn't create my own patchwork spirituality nor did I try to invent my own religious practice. I initially set out to find a spiritual tradition so that I would have someone to guide me to progress on the path.

---

[32] "The path finds you" is a common expression among many spiritual teachings, in my experience many seekers do have the experience of being found by their path.

Creating my own faith would defeat my original purpose for embarking on this project to begin with. I had observed people who had created their own spiritual path and I felt there was an essential loneliness to not sharing your journey with others. Fully committing to path helps to create commitment and accountability. It provides resources which I couldn't get curating my own path. On an energetic level, I have observed that creating my own path caused my energy to diffuse and spread out much as rivers do when they empty into a delta. My spiritual practice can become indistinct and powerless without the guidance of a teacher or a community. Having leaders and teachers provides structure and gives me someone to answer my questions. Part of the reason for my search was to find someone or something outside of myself to enlarge my spiritual life. This is not to say that I don't appreciate or incorporate things I have learned from other traditions. I consider it a privilege to know so much about so many faiths. This, however, is what Hannah's real wisdom was: *Pick a bus.* Don't watch them go by and rationalize why you don't want to go to this destination or that destination. Earnestly pursue a spiritual experience and grow your spiritual life. Sure, you can sit on a bench, check the route maps, select a destination and talk to other passengers, but you won't go anywhere until you get on a bus.

Taming that B*tch in Your Head

The epicenter of all shame is self-hatred. For me it fueled all of my actions and thoughts. I was profoundly uncomfortable in my own skin. I felt that I wasn't smart enough, that my family wasn't rich enough, that my hips were too big and my nose was too flat. I committed innumerable hours to trying to change things I was ashamed and couldn't change.

I listened daily to what my friend Jonna calls, 'that bitch inside my head.' It was like a radio station that broadcast negative messages day and night. *You'll probably screw this up... no one will ever love you ... you aren't as pretty as she is...they'll figure out you're faking...* and on and on. I listened to this voice and tried to adjust, and just like a golfer trying too hard to adjust their swing, my situation simply got worse and worse.

My professional success was predicated almost entirely on proving that I wasn't an impostor. I spent countless hours strategizing on how to hide that fact that I didn't know, that I wasn't smart enough, that I couldn't do something that was expected of me. As a result, I was constantly exhausted by the efforts of an ordinary workday. Reflecting back, I see that many of the people who I saw succeed did so because they believed in themselves. At some point, they understood that they had to be their own cheerleader.

I believe much of my behavior with food welled up from this self-hatred. Like many addicts, I used food to numb myself and to shut down the incessant stream of self-criticism. I over-exercised to the point of injuring myself and starved myself as a punishment for all my perceived failures. My first year of college I worried constantly that I would I flunk out. I really believed that I didn't belong there and I wasn't as good as the other students. I resorted to a cycle of bingeing and starving. I would go for days without eating or run until I was exhausted and the thought in my head was, *you deserve this because you really suck.* It saddens me now to recognize the cruelty of my own thinking but, I went on like this for another 20 years.

It is easy to envision being gentle and patient with a child. As parents, we allow our kids to make mistakes and ask questions. We also make sure they get rest when they are tired or eat well before going to school. This kind of care for children seems obvious, yet we are often unable to give ourselves the same simple kindness. Kindness to myself proved to be the road to recovering from perfectionism.

Recovery, like gardening, requires constant attention to prevent weeds from springing up. I first clearly saw my own self-hatred when in therapy. My therapist pointed out the number of times I said negative things about myself and asked me why I spoke to myself so unkindly. Initially, I found the question ridiculous because I had never been without this endless stream of negative thoughts. Over time I began to wonder, *Was there another way for me to think? Was there another way for me to live?* I did learn to overcome the self-hate. Below is a summary of some of the tools that I found helpful, these can be a starting point for your journey.

Personal Inventory

There are two other powerful tools I learned to use that helped roll back the habit of self-hatred and negative self- talk. First, I took a personal inventory[33] of my resentments and failures. This led me surprisingly to the conclusion that I was just an ordinary human being who was prone to selfishness, greed, envy, and pride just like the rest of humanity throughout history. Through this inventory, I recognized as the bible says 'there is nothing new under the sun.[34]' My life

---

[33] This process is known in 12 step programs as the Fourth Step inventory. More detail on this process can be found in The Alcoholics Anonymous Book popularly known as 'The Big Book.' There are also a number of workbooks and guides on conducting this process in the recovery community. See the back of this book for additional resources.

[34] Ecclesiastes 1:9

isn't all that extraordinary. My suffering isn't some kind of special suffering and my mistakes are by no means unique. It sounds counter-intuitive but this helped me realize that I was just one human being doing my best to get along. I wasn't particularly better than or worse than other people.

A personal inventory is a list of resentments and fears. The way I did this was by making a chronological list of all my resentments. Then I went back through the list and wrote a narrative of exactly what happened and what resentment I associated with the event.

For example:

JONI B. EXCLUDED ME FROM THE GIRLS GROUP ON OUR STREET. SHE WOULDN'T LET THE OTHER GIRLS WALK TO SCHOOL WITH ME AND SNUBBED ME ON THE PLAYGROUND.

RESENTMENT: HURT MY PRIDE, MADE ME FEEL LIKE NOT ENOUGH, MADE IT HARD FOR ME TO MAKE OTHER FRIENDS, MADE ME SUSPECT OTHER GIRLS

I found that doing this as thoroughly as possible made it more effective. It is important to treat it like an inventory, just counting up and collecting resentments in one place, not blaming or revisiting the pain of the experiences. It also wasn't helpful for me to spend time blaming the other person for their part. As a friend once said, "Yes, they did something to hurt you but you're the one who is still carrying it around."

I found it helpful to read it to someone else. It diffused the shame I felt about the incident. Finding someone to read this to can be tricky. Use the same guidelines here as recommended in the chapter *Firing the Committee*. Clerics and therapists take an oath of confidentiality so they are good candidates but only if they listen without trying to offer advice. The important thing is to be heard, not fixed.

As an on-going practice, I try to keep my accounts short. When I make a mistake, I try to apologize promptly rather than let my actions fuel a sense of shame. Since doing an inventory I feel that I have a saner assessment of what I can and can't do. I also acknowledge my short comings and try to stay out of situations that might trigger them. I am prone to greed and envy so I try to avoid conversations about pricey neighborhoods and expensive cars. I know that I have a tendency to try to control situations so I now decline to take leadership roles without careful consideration. I find that knowing myself helps prevent getting into difficult and painful situations. I understand now that much of the pain that I experience is self-inflicted. Self-knowledge has allowed me the freedom to live with others with much less stress, anxiety and conflict. I don't cause myself so much trouble because *I know what causes me trouble.*

The Practice of Meditation

There are many forms of meditation and many more opinions about it. My view of meditation is that it is the simple act of training my mind to stay in the present moment. As human beings, we all seem to find this very difficult. We are not really wired for living in either the past or the future. Our senses are acutely tuned to living in the present, we connect with the phenomenal world through sight, sound, smell, taste, and touch. Every moment is a sumptuous feast which we mostly miss because we are carrying on a relentless internal conversation. Learning to meditate helped me immensely with my ability to stay in the present. The habit of staying in the present in turn provided a bonanza of clarity, joy, patience, tolerance and compassion. I am a different person today because I meditate.

Meditation also involves learning to sit with the discomfort of feelings. I was amazed to discover that both anger and craving pass in under two minutes. As one friend of mine says, "Feel the feeling now or feel it later with interest." In meditation, I also discovered my tendency to numb my feelings, particularly negative feelings. I realized that when I felt unhappy, frightened or anxious I would find something, outside of myself, to reduce the feeling. This could be a glass of wine, a television show, a chocolate bar or a new pair of shoes. Meditation taught me to stay with the feeling and to sit with it without running away or trying to turn it off. The completely unexpected consequence was that I enjoy life infinitely more than I used to. I notice things I never used to notice like the wind on my face or the extraordinary color of my friend's eyes or the sweetness in a carrot. I'm not barreling through life, talking to myself and avoiding feeling anything.

It would be hard to exaggerate the power this simple practice has had on my life. Initially, I meditated for 5 minutes once a week. During those brief moments of sitting still, a habit that initially was completely foreign to me, I found an unfamiliar sense of peace. Around this same time, I embarked on what I would describe as a quest for a spiritual path. I recognized the feeling of an internal void and a hunger for spiritual expression. This journey eventually led to the discovery of the teachings of Chogyam Trungpa Rinpoche and number of other realized meditation masters. Gradually, I learned the simple, profound practice of meditation.

Over time, I increased my practice to at least 20 minutes a day. When I have time, I sit for 40 minutes to an hour a day. I go on regular community retreats and eventually took annual solitary retreats. The accumulated hours of meditation began to wear away at the veneer of my negative view of myself. As time went on I saw that the nature of my mind was naturally strong and spacious. Far from the claustrophobic ranting of my daily life I discovered I had a kind of innate serenity and wholesomeness that was obscured by my obsessive thoughts. Gradually, I began to be gentler with myself in a way that seemed nearly magical. As an unexpected bonus, I became gentler and more forgiving with those around me. Another benefit is that I experience an increased acuity about the world around me. I feel the pulse of a drumbeat, notice the smell of jasmine in the air, and feel the anxiety of my neighbor when he talks about his teenage son. It is as if I feel more alive and I find life in the present moment more enjoyable.

One valuable principle I learned in meditation is to lean into the feeling. For most of my life I avoided pain or negative emotions. If I felt angry I would try to suppress it, if I felt fear I would brush it aside. This habit had become so natural that I didn't realize how regularly I felt nothing at all no matter what happened, good or bad. In meditation I learned to just experience what was happening. A simple example is acknowledging that my nose is itching and exploring the feeling of an itch.

From my personal experience, I highly recommend joining a community to meditate. Meditation is traditionally taught on a one-to-one basis with a teacher transmitting the instructions and sharing their own experience with a student. Meditation is much more likely to help you with shame if you seek out personal meditation instruction. Experiencing your own mind can be thrilling, but it can also be frightening and perplexing. Having someone to guide you through the process of learning to meditate is both important and helpful. Trying it on your own may not have the same results. I learned to meditate by attending classes at the Shambhala Meditation Center. Many meditation centers offer comparable beginning meditation classes.

It is a common misconception that meditation will free you from thinking or transport you to some remarkable spiritual dimension. This has not been my experience. I have found that my mind is still pretty chatty, with both negative and positive thoughts. I have had a few experiences of feeling lifted into a spiritual dimension but these have been the exception and not the rule. The benefit I have received from practicing daily meditation is a sense of profound serenity and an increased ability to stay present in the moment. My gradual acceptance of myself has led to a feeling of gratitude and joy. Most days I like being in my own company, I enjoy my life and I feel compassion and kindness towards myself and those around me.

Over time I have become more familiar with my own mind. I see the ways it darts around, looking for something to attach to. I see how it hungers for something to happen, for some new drama to erupt. I also see the ways in which it strong and genuine. Overcoming shame has in part been the result of the emergence of my own authenticity. Meditation led me to see who I really am and to have a sane assessment of my strengths and weaknesses. Meditation taught me how to relax and be myself. When I am meditating regularly I find that things don't get under my skin and I'm comfortable with who I am and how I respond to situations. It seems like there are fewer instances in which I feel I have done something wrong.

Over the years I have been inconsistent in my practice. I go through periods where I meditate daily. I have had periods where I meditated for hours a day or gone on retreat several times a year. I have also had periods where I haven't been able to meditate for weeks or months. I accept these as part of the ups and downs of life. What I have learned is that my personal sense of well-being, my ability to cope with daily life and my ability to be present and authentic is greatly enhanced by daily meditation. Not meditating doesn't make me a bad girl, it's more like a missed opportunity or a resource that I haven't made use of. The important thing for me has been not to turn it into another reason for shaming myself.

My meditation practice has changed over the years as a result of learning new practices and becoming more mentally grounded. One thing I know for certain is that consistency trumps quantity. I have found it is better to sit daily, even if only for five minutes than it is for me to be able to practice for a longer session. In my experience that 'daily-ness' of practice has the most profound impact.

There are numerous methods of meditation.

They vary by spiritual tradition and origin. You can place your attention on different objects, chants or images. Many people have found meditative activities like working on puzzles or coloring[35]helpful. There are forms of Christian, Buddhist, and Hindu meditation to name only a few. My personal preference is the practice of shamatha which places the attention on the breath because my breath is always with me. At any moment during my workday or at home I can place my attention on my breath without having to formally meditate. For me the point is that meditation is a powerful tool in diffusing shame. Searching for the right meditation practice can be an adventure, but the important thing is to be consistent with the practice you choose.

I've read a number of books I found helpful including *The Art of Happiness* by the Dalai Lama, *The Sacred Path of the Warrior* by Chogyam Trungpa Rinpoche, *The Book* by Alan Watts, and *Zen Mind Beginners Mind* by Suzuki Roshi.

I've found a number of audio books to be extremely useful. For helping me with the

---

Because I found so many people have difficulty starting to meditate I created a contemplative coloring book, *The Fabled Land*, as a way to begin to meditate. Purchase this book at TheLoveMandala.com or at StephanieMillerArtist.com.

physical parts of meditation practice I appreciated the instruction provided by Dr. Reginald Ray in *Meditating with the Body*. For understanding the nature of ego, I like Ekhardt Tolle's *Stillness Speaks*. I have also listened to many of Pema Chodron's teachings in particular I like her brief series *Getting Unstuck* and the lengthier teachings in *Noble Heart*. The gift of living in the West is that all of these resources are readily available to us. It is our extreme good fortune that many of the Tibetan masters and their students came to English speaking countries as they fled the Chinese invasion. The teachings of thousands of great meditation instructors are readily available in most libraries, in bookstores and on-line[36].

The Practice of Gratitude

I'm not proud to admit how much I used to dislike it when people told me to have gratitude. I labeled it a new age fad and I felt like I was exempt from needing to feel grateful for both large and small gifts in my life.

My spiritual teacher challenged this assumption and suggested that I try making a list of things I was grateful for. She also encouraged me to look for things to be grateful for even in trying

---

[36] In order to make these resources easier to find I have made them available for sale on our website under RESOURCES at TheLoveMandala.com.

circumstances. I had to admit that she seemed to have a consistently positive and serene world view so I finally tried it. I was amazed what a difference it made to look for something to be grateful for. Suddenly the world seemed kinder to me and I realized how much I depended on others every single day. I could be grateful to the farmers who grew my food and the checker who rung up my order. Later I began to recognize the bounty of the earth, the soil, the rain and the life that sprung from it.

Another friend challenged me to make a list of a thousand things I was grateful for and it opened my eyes to how truly fortunate I am. Gratitude turned my attention away from envy and selfishness. It became a universal solvent for the sticky, painful and difficult problems and feelings that had plagued me for years. Even more miraculous was the way in which it transformed my obsession with food and weight loss. Experiencing a feeling of gratitude helped diffuse the anxiety and discomfort that often caused me to eat or starve. It also transformed my relationship with my body from being critical to grateful.

The Fine Art of Self-Care

Our society is one that is predicated on accomplishment, add to this the speed at which we do things and acquire information and we find ourselves on a never-ending treadmill of activity. Few of us take time out of our busy schedules to care for ourselves and our bodies. In fact, the idea of self-care is sometimes looked upon as an indulgence in our culture. We admire people who get regular exercise because that is an accomplishment, but a woman who gets regular facials or manicures might be derided as vain. Self-care is also undercut by our lack of knowledge about the practice of self-care and our own bodies. Most of us don't know how much sleep we really need, what foods make us tired or irritable or when our schedules are too full.

My therapist asked me what was I doing to take care of myself. I said, "Going to work to pay for expenses." What I was really saying was, "I don't know what self-care is." Then she gently explained that self-care was a way of loving myself. *Could I take a hot bath, get a massage, spend an afternoon with a girlfriend?* I quickly realized that what she suggested were things I considered luxuries. I would only indulge myself when I felt I could afford the time. Now, many years later, I have come to understand that self-care is not only essential but that it supports my ability to do all the other things in my life. My therapist encouraged me to buy some really nice body cream and thoroughly moisturize my skin after I showered. As my first conscious act of self-care I carefully covered my whole body (even the spaces between my toes) with body butter. In that moment, I felt the pleasure of caring for all the parts of my body I had ignored.

I have found that many of my friends have a

similar response when I ask them about self-care. They either consider self-care superfluous or they don't even understand the concept. The situation is particularly acute for caretakers, mothers and others whose job it is to care for others. They spend so much time taking care of loved ones they've forgotten how to care for themselves.

Cultivating self-care is an art. It begins with knowing myself and my body. In the course of recovering from my eating disorders I discovered that I didn't handle sugar, caffeine or wheat products very well. I came to understand that some of my emotional disturbances came from low blood sugar and that I functioned better when I didn't allow it to drop precipitously. For me this means I need to eat every four to five hours. My lifelong habit of skipping lunch or grabbing whatever I could eat on the go with no planning didn't really work for me. One of the most furious arguments I ever had with my husband was after I hadn't eaten all day.

Self-care requires me to pay attention to my body and my emotional state. It also requires me to slow down and make boundaries. I struggled with saying "Yes" to things I didn't really want to do or cramming my schedule full because I was afraid of missing something. One of my first acts of self-care was learning to say "No." Later, I also learned to say "No" without providing excuses or explanations. *I don't want to be a member of the board for a professional organization, I've done that and I didn't like it.* Of course, I could provide value and can visualize all the things I could do. It doesn't mean I have to add another commitment to my schedule. I don't have to go to a business party after work or a drive a friend to LAX on Friday night. For years, I didn't understand that just because someone asked didn't mean I had to do it. It isn't an excuse to be selfish, it is a sane assessment of what I can and can't do.

One of the main obstacles to self-care is paradoxically the shame we feel about doing it. Most of us think that taking an hour for a hot bath is wasting time. We don't plan self-care into our schedules because we don't feel that it is legitimate to do so. The first, and most important step, is becoming willing to take care of yourself. The second is making self-care a priority.

As I explored self-care I realized that I really needed eight hours of sleep to be at my best. As a lifelong night owl, the idea of getting in bed at 9:00 seemed ridiculous, but as soon as I started getting more sleep I felt so much better. I realized the reason I stayed up late was often to watch television or tinker on the computer, which wasn't really productive. Now one of my favorite parts of my day is going to bed early, and reading. Another discovery I made was the power of the cat nap. Even on busy days I sometimes set an alarm and lay down for 20 minutes. It's amazing how creating a little space for a nap can be so relaxing and refreshing.

One of the powerful acts of self-care for me has been learning to take advantage of the many forms of bodywork available. I have found tremendous recovery from yoga, massage and pilates. I have also visited shen, reiki and breath therapists and participated in other forms of healing. I readily admit that these practices are not for everyone. Some people believe they are genuinely powerful and others believe that they are a sham. Personally, I approached these practices with extreme skepticism and was surprised by their effectiveness.

I suffered from back pain continuously for nine months. During that time, I went to the doctor repeatedly and eventually tried a chiropractor. Nothing helped and after months of being unable to sleep comfortably, drive, or sit for any length of time I became desperate. A friend suggested I try massage. The massage therapist suggested that my issues weren't physical and that I needed to address some emotional issues. When I said I was seeing a therapist she said, somewhat grimly, "Talking won't help." Eventually I visited a shen therapist who unlocked a reservoir of grief from my childhood. My back pain went away the following day. I can't explain it, but I know, in my case, it helped when nothing else seemed to work.

At one point, I had what a friend calls 'the herd of people who take care of me.' I had a therapist, a massage therapist, a chiropractor, a doctor, a pilates instructor, a mentor, a meditation instructor and whole crew of friends who helped me recover from my eating disorders. It was what I needed at the time, and though I was embarrassed by the number of people I relied on, I doubt I would have recovered without their help. Recovering from shame meant being willing to use all the resources it took, even if it felt indulgent. After years of self-hatred and self-abuse developing a practice of paying attention to myself and attending to my needs was a difficult but necessary change.

Talismans

Along with bodywork I have also found talismans to be an extremely helpful way to help with my recovery. So much of our time is taken up by thinking, words and concepts but the problem of shame is, in many ways, non-conceptual. By that I mean that it is a feeling not a concrete idea. This is why talismans can be so powerful. Talismans can function as a reminder but they can also help you to feel imbued with courage and strength. The key is that a talisman functions as a symbol of something larger, perhaps something you can't articulate in words.

You may already be using some kind of talisman. It can be a piece of jewelry from someone who loves and supports you or a picture or place or a time in your life when you felt strong or happy or loved. The point is not to be attached to an object but to feel empowered by that object and to appreciate your own natural inner strength.

When my friend's mother died one of her aunts gave her five smooth stones, which is what David used to kill Goliath in the Bible. She felt that these stones gave her power as they had given David. My girlfriend gave me of five smooth stones when I was going through a difficult time and I still have them 10 years later. My smooth stones give me a sense of power and remind me that I don't have to do things alone.

I have a small raven on my desk. In Native American lore, the raven communes with the unknown and carries messages from the void. Whenever I feel uninspired or confused I look to my raven knowing that something magical can arise at any moment. I always feel relieved knowing that the raven is there. As often as not, my mind relaxes and I am able to move forward.

It is important not to view your talismans as some kind of magical object. It should function as a symbol and a reminder. It should make you feel good to have it, but not panicked when you don't. Try to avoid the pitfalls inherent in having lucky socks or some other talisman that makes you feel incomplete when you don't have it. You don't want to be in situation of feel devastated by the loss of talisman.

The Positive Evidence Locker

I've found that I'm much better at remembering insults and failures than I am at remembering victories. That's why I created the Positive

Evidence Locker. It's a place where I write down good things that happen to me, compliments and other important evidence that indicates how I'm taken care every day.

Maintaining my own Positive Evidence Locker has improved my ability to experience gratitude. Noticing the ways that things turned out well helps me to believe they will turn out well again. Sometimes I even record other people's Positive Evidence just to remind me how miraculous the world can be. When one of my friends was expanding her business she needed a large sum of money in order to renovate a new space. She felt confident it was the right move but she didn't know how to fund it. She made a list of all the ways she could make the extra money without having to go into debt. Out of the blue an advertising agency contacted her about doing a commercial in Japan, even though she wasn't actively pursuing making commercials. She went on an all-expenses-paid trip to Japan and was able to cover the cost of her renovation with the income from the commercial. I love this story because it reminds me how abundant the universe is and how I can be supported from unexpected quarters.

You can start your Positive Evidence Locker by creating a list in an ordinary notebook. Write a sentence or two to remind you of what happened so you'll remember later. My entries look like this:

1) HAVING THE MONEY TO REPLACE THE KITCHEN COUNTERS

2) GETTING ON THE ONLY FLIGHT TO IRELAND THAT WASN'T CANCELLED WHEN MOM FELL

3) FINDING THE MISMARKED RAINCOAT IN MY SIZE FOR $65 WHEN ALL THE OTHER ONES WERE $175

4) THE TV COMMERCIAL TO HELP FUND JENN'S STORE

Each of these are stories that remind me that things usually work out for me and for people I know. When I'm feeling like a victim or a failure my Positive Evidence Locker can pull me out of a negative feeling and reframe my experience.

The God Box

Sometimes I just can't let go of things. During the recession, my husband and I were both out of work. I worried incessantly about how we would pay our bills. I couldn't let go of my fear of being a bag lady. A friend of mine suggested I try a God Box, all I needed to do was write my worries down and put them in the box for God to take care of. If you aren't comfortable with the idea of God you can make a Spirit Box, or the Abundant Universe Box. The main thing is to surrender to the fact that you are not all powerful and something larger than you is at work. At first, I felt silly writing down the seemingly trivial things that I was worried about. Over time I realized that I got real relief and stopped worrying about the things I put in my God Box. When I emptied the God Box out a few years later I was amazed to discover that almost all my worries had, in fact, been taken care of. It's a great practice to empty out the box and see how many of you worries were unfounded or turned out totally fine.

I like writing with a good old-fashioned pen on a piece of paper but there are also God Box apps for your phone.

The Hardest Step of All

The process of befriending myself has been a slow one. It wasn't as if I got up one day and suddenly liked myself. It was a slow, steady process of trying to be kinder to myself and appreciate myself as I am.

One extremely powerful technique I learned from a friend was to look myself in the eye in the mirror and to say, "I love you Stephanie." Of the many practices, I have suggested this one was the hardest for me. I was often overcome with a feeling of hatred or shame when I look in the mirror. I had to learn to combat this habit by doing the exact opposite. I did this daily for at least two years before I stopped loathing the process. I thought of it like taking vitamins or cleaning toilets, just something I had to get done. One day I noticed that I didn't feel so uncomfortable anymore. I felt the gradual loosening of that shame and criticism. I realized that I was grateful for the clear, olive skin that my mother had, the natural curl to my hair, the height that once hated. I still struggle with picking at my flaws when I look in the mirror, but if I take a breath and remember that I am my own best friend I can feel a softening in my heart.

By becoming my own best friend, I've learned to help myself feel better about me. I picture one of those common scenes in coming-of-age movies. The sidekick is laying on the bed in a teen bedroom encouraging the heroine to go to the prom/run for election/challenge the teacher and the best friend always believes in the heroine. Now I'm my own sidekick. I believe the best about me. Try practicing the art of being your own sidekick. Tell yourself, *you can totally do this, you're completely awesome, go for it* and then practice believing it.

I found all of these tools to be helpful in my recovery. Most of them were given to me by someone else. I've found it a good practice to ask people what they do to take care of themselves. If you have someone you admire or who seems comfortable with themselves try asking them what they do. It's a good way to spark conversation and it may lead to helping you feel good.

108 Ways to Feel Better

There are times when I feel like I need a little self-care but I can't think of what to do. I offer this list to inspire you with ideas on how to start.

1. Ask your friends what they like about you

2. Book time your calendar just for yourself

3. Book an appointment to go to a movie, concert or event you enjoy with a special friend

4. Buy a nice body butter and apply it slowly and carefully, pay attention to your forgotten parts like elbows, heels and ankles

5. Buy a plant for your house

6. Buy a sugar or salt exfoliating scrub and put it next to your bathroom sink. Every few days give your hands a one-minute spa treatment.

7. Buy soap in a beautiful fragrance to use in your kitchen

8. Buy tickets to see your favorite band live

9. Buy yourself fancy chocolates

10. Buy yourself flowers

11. Buy yourself something you've always wanted and wrap it to open later

12. Call a friend you haven't spoken to in a while.

13. Dance

14. Deep condition your hair

15. Do nothing

16. Do something that feels totally extravagant

17. Draw something, even if you aren't an "artist"

18. Drive a different route to work

19. Eat breakfast

20. Eat dessert first

21. Floss, take vitamins and wear sunscreen

22. Get a massage, facial, manicure or pedicure

23. Get your car washed

24. Go ahead and order a decadent meal

25. Go for a bicycle ride

26. Go for a swim in a lake or the ocean

27. Go on shopping trip to buy yourself new underwear, socks and pajamas then throw out the old ones

28. Go someplace you've never been

29. Go to a plant nursery and smell flowers

30. Go to bed early

31. Go to a museum

32. Go to the doctor when you're sick, take medicine and sleep

33. Go to the movies

34. Have a routine physical and follow up on the required tests

35. Hire a professional personal stylist or home decorator for a consultation

36. Hire someone to clean your house before a party

37. Hug yourself and rub your upper arms

38. Invite your five-favorite people out for an inexpensive outing

39. Just do one thing and then rest

40. Keep a gratitude list

41. Keep a list of 100 things you love

42. Lay down for 5 minutes and put a warm, damp cloth on your face or a lavender pillow over your eyes

43. Lay down on the couch, prop your feet up and read something printed on paper like a magazine or a book.

44. Learn to do something new

45. Learn to say "No"

46. Listen to your intuition

47. Look up free events in your area and attend

48. Look yourself in the eye in the mirror

49. Let something go, for an hour or even a whole day. Don't make your bed, don't do the laundry, skip taking care of everyone else.

50. Make yourself a cup of tea or cocoa, sit down and sip it

51. Meditate

52. Pick flowers and make an arrangement for your house

53. Plan a staycation

54. Plant flowers in the front yard (bulbs are great because they'll surprise you later when they come up)

55. Play music

56. Play on the swings

57. Play with your pet

58. Read poetry

59. Repair something that's broken

60. Send a card to someone you love for no special reason

61. Set the dinner table with candles and play soft music

62. Shop in a store you've never been to

63. Sing

64. Sit by a fireplace, fire-pit or in the sun and feel the warmth

65. Sit in your yard and watch birds

66. Skip

67. Sleep in

68. Speak up for yourself

69. Spend 10 minutes cleaning out a messy drawer or cabinet shelf

70. Stay in your pajamas all day and watch old movies

71. Stretch

72. Take a class that's non-essential but has always interested you

73. Take a day off work for no reason

74. Take a five-minute walk

75. Take a hot bath with Epsom salts and scented bubble bath

76. Take a nap

77. Take a restorative yoga class

78. Take three deep breaths

79. Tell someone you love them

80. Throw away stuff that's broken and you can't fix

81. Turn off your phone and put away your computer for an hour (or a DAY!)

82. Walk in nature

83. Watch something funny (I love old Carol Burnett episodes)

84. Wear something that makes you feel strong

85. Wrap yourself in a big soft blanket

86. Write a song

87. Write in your journal

88. Use a pen and add to this list with your own ideas (yes, a pen, I know it's killing you)

89.

90.

91.

92.

93.

94.

95.

96.

97.

98.

99.

100.

101.

102.

103.

104.

105.

106.

107.

108.

You can also ask other people what they do for self-care. People often have novel ideas. You can find ways to encourage yourself to do more self-care[37]. I randomly draw a card from my card deck of homemade spa treatments. Make a self-care date on your calendar or ask a friend to do something with you. Try picking a few of these that appeal to you and experiment with self-care.

Another form of self-care can be taking up a

---

[37] Please email me your self-care ideas so I can share them with others, Stephanie@TheLoveMandala.com.

hobby. I always wanted to try archery and I finally did when I was in my 40s. I loved it just I always thought I would. One of my friends says, 'follow sparkly bread crumbs', if something gets your attention follow it. The feeling of learning something new or doing something you love can be very curative.

Now, Try Getting a C+

If you're anything like me, you have big plans now that you've finished this book. You're going to turn over a new leaf and be the best recovered perfectionist ever. You're going to buy a fresh, new notebook and do all the exercises I've suggested. I'd like to invite you to try something new, don't make this a new project. Don't compete with yourself. Don't create a new impossible finish line. That's what I would do, but, I suggest you try something different.

Now is the time to learn to be gentle and make friends with yourself. Notice how hard you've been on yourself and forgive yourself. Then, go out and try doing something poorly, or doing nothing at all. Recovering from the shame that has crippled you for years or decades won't happen overnight. It begins with this simple, single step: Being gentle with you. Give up the playing tricks and games with yourself and just be *you* with all your flaws. You may be surprised to discover how profoundly perfect you are right now, in this very moment.

Be well.

Join the Dance

Not some engraved invitation
Comes to this besieged heart
Whirling, amidst chaos
I see them beyond sorrow and joy
Hope and fear
Tears streaming and collapse
Inside the union of lover and beloved
The silent come-on, an open hand
Incline of the head, languorous nod
Then backs turned, chins up, spinning
I am welcome any time
Every time
What do I withhold?
With my prudish 'No'
My wallflower habit
Fear of rejection
And hope of perfection
Since dancers began
I have demurred at invitations
Or expected none
Now, at last, on the cusp of the mean
I understand that there is always an invitation
That the dance floor
Is an equal partner to every Dancer
And I have only to join in,
For the darkness to depart
To fly free
And spare myself the pain
Of not joining
The dance given in my honor

Acknowledgements

It has been my good fortune to have wonderful friends and family who have supported and encouraged me, even during the dark days of my dis-ease and recovery. If I tried to name them all this book would go on for another 200 pages. There are a few people who were instrumental in this project. Thank you to Martine Bouman for the original inspiration to write this book. I owe deep gratitude to Jodie George, Sam West, Rhoda Pell, Clare deCheneau, Alex Davis, and Jonna Fries for the vital lessons that changed my life. To Carolyn Kanjuro, Daniel Krog, Giavanni Washington and especially Will Brand for reading this manuscript, editing and making excellent contributions. Thank you to the Girl Geniuses for your belief in me every step of the way. My heartfelt gratitude to Laura Biswas who has been a support, a sounding board and most of all a midwife in bringing this book to life.

Finally, thank you to my husband who has been a confidant, friend, lover, teacher, editor and cat wrangler throughout this process. Without his steadfast love, I would never have had the courage to face and conquer the shame that bound me for so many years.

This is a list of organizations, websites, podcasts and books that may be helpful on your journey to self-love and acceptance. Many of these resources are available on our website TheLoveMandala.com under "Resources".

Addiction

AlAnon
1600 Corporate Landing Parkway
Virginia Beach, VA 23454-5617
Telephone: (757) 563-1600
Fax: (757) 563-1656
Email: **wso@al-anon.org**
Toll-free Meeting Line: (888) 425-2666
AlAnon.org

Alcoholics Anonymous
A.A. World Services, Inc.
P.O. Box 459,
Grand Central Station
New York, NY 10163
(212) 870-3400
AA.org

Adult Children of Alcoholics
ACA WSO
Post Office Box 811
Lakewood, CA 90714 USA
310-534-1815
AdultChildren.org

Debtors Anonymous
PO Box 920888
Needham, MA 02492-0009
800-421-2383
DebtorsAnonymous.org

Gamblers Anonymous
International Service Office
P.O. Box 17173
Los Angeles, CA 90017
T (626) 960-3500
F (626) 960-3501
isomain@gamblersanonymous.org
GamblersAnonymous.org

Narcotics Anonymous
NA World Services
PO Box 9999
Van Nuys, California USA 91409
Telephone +1.818.773.9999
Fax +1.818.700.0700
NA.org

Overeaters Anonymous
PO Box 44020
Rio Rancho, New Mexico 87174-4020 USA
505-891-2664
OA.org

Sex and Love Addicts Anonymous
1550 NE Loop 410 Suite 118
San Antonio, TX 78209 USA
210-828-7900
SLAAfws.org

Beattie, Melody. *Language of Letting Go*. Hay
House Inc, 2005.

Rehab Reviews – Reviews of over 7,000 rehab
centers, referrals for therapists, legal services and
sober living facilities
RehabReviews.com

Hazelden Betty Ford Foundation
HazeldenBettyFord.org

Hazelden Publishing – resources for people
suffering from addiction and their loved ones
Hazelden.org

TED (Technology, Entertainment and Design)
Ideas Worth Spreading – Curated TED talks on
the topic of addiction
TED.com/topics/addiction

Help.org – A listing of the best rehab facilities for
those on a budget and the most luxurious
facilities for those who desire the exclusivity and
convenience they provide.
Help.org

Eating Disorders

Gay, Roxane. *Hunger: A Memoir of (My) Body.*
Corsair, 2018.
UCLA Eating Disorders Program
UCLAHealth.org/EatingDisorders/

Rosewood Centers for Eating Disorders
RosewoodRanch.com

NEDA
NationalEatingDisorders.org

Financial

Dave Ramsey
Ramsey Solutions
1749 Mallory Lane
Brentwood, TN 37027
General:
888.227.3223
Financial Peace University 877-378-2667
DaveRamsey.com

Marie Forleo – coaches on wealth mindset
MarieForleo.com

Hill, Napoleon. *Think and Grow Rich: The
Complete Classic Text.* Jeremy P.
Tarcher/Penguin, 2008.

Gender and Sexual Identity

Los Angeles LGBT Center - resources for lesbian, gay, bi-sexual and transgendered people **LALGBTCenter.org**

Trans* Lounge Program Library – classes for lesbian, gay, bi-sexual and transgendered people **TransLoung.org**

Transgender Law Center – legal assistance for lesbian, gay, bi-sexual and transgendered people **TransgenderLawCenter.org**

Downs, Alan. *The Velvet Rage: Overcoming the Pain of Growing up Gay in a Straight Man's World.* Da Capo Life Long, 2012.

Mindfulness and Meditation

Chodron, Pema. *Living Beautifully: with Uncertainty and Change.* Shambhala, 2015.

Hanh, Thich Nhat. *Art of Living: Peace and Freedom in the Here and Now.* Harper One, 2018.

Kornfield, Jack. *After the Ecstasy, the Laundry: How the Heart Grows Wise on the Spiritual Path*. Bantam Books, 2001

Lama, Dalai, and Howard C. Cutler. *The Art of Happiness*. Hachette Australia, 2018.

Ponlop, Dzogchen. *Emotional Rescue: How to Work with Your Emotions to Transform Hurt and Confusion into Energy That Empowers You*. Penguin Books, 2017.

Ray, Reginald A. *Touching Enlightenment: Finding Realization in the Body*. Sounds True, 2014.

Simmer-Brown, Judith. Dakini's *Warm Breath: The Feminine Principle in Tibetan Buddhism*. Shambhala, 2003.

Suzuki, Shunryu, et al. *Zen Mind, Beginner's Mind*. Shambhala, 2011.

Tolle, Eckhart. *Stillness Speaks: Whispers of Now*. Hodder, 2011.

Tolle, Eckhart. *The Power of Now: A Guide to Spiritual Enlightenment*. Hachette Australia, 2008.

Trungpa, Chogyam. *Shambhala: The Sacred Path of the Warrior*. Random House Inc., 2015.

Sounds True is a resource for books and recordings on meditation.
SoundsTrue.com

Shambhala Publications is an excellent resource for books and teachings on meditation, mindfulness, wellness, psychology and religion
Shambhala.com

Dr. Reginald Ray is good at helping you to connect with your body in the practice of meditation
DharmaOcean.org

Trime Lhawang (Patrick Sweeney) is a Western teacher in the Karma Kagyu lineage of Tibetan Buddhist, his teaching are intellectually stimulating and include some physical practices like Qigong and yoga.
Satdharma.com

Zenko Kyudojo – Zen archery in the lineage of Shibata Sensei
ZenkoInternational.org

Personal Transformation

Fleet Maull – Teaches on the concept of radical responsibility ™ and rejecting the victim paradigm
FleetMaull.com

Hendricks, Gay. *The Big Leap: Conquer Your Hidden Fear and Take Life to the Next Level.* HarperCollins, 2010.

LaPorte, Danielle *The Desire Map: A Guide to Creating Goals with Soul* Sounds True Inc., 2014

Physical Healing

Ackerman, Diane. *Natural History of the Senses.* Vintage, 1991.

Hay, Louise L. *You Can Heal Your Life.* Hay House, 2008.

Kraftsow, Gary. *Yoga for Wellness: Healing with the Timeless Teachings of Viniyoga.* Penguin Books, 1999

Myss, Caroline M. *Anatomy of the Spirit: The Seven Stages of Power and Healing.* Sydney, 1997.

Palmer, Wendy. *The Intuitive Body: Discovering the Wisdom of Conscious Embodiment and Aikido.* Blue Snake Books, 2008.

Ray, Reginald A. *The Awakening Body: Somatic Meditation for Discovering Our Deepest Life.* Shambhala, 2016.

Eva Wong – teaches Taoist qigong a spiritual discipline that cultivates body and mind simultaneously
LimitlessGate.com

Sharon Jakubecy Klehm - Alexander Technique and Art of Breathing teacher helping women heighten awareness of their body, breath, and voice so they can release traumatic tension and body blocks and discover the open, confident, and energized body they live in and their resonant, powerful voice in front of any audience.
 AlexanderTechniqueLA.com

Psychology

Bradshaw, John. *Healing the Shame That Binds You.* Health Communications, 2005.

Brown, Brene. *Daring Greatly: How the Courage to Be Vulnerable Transforms the Way We Live, Love, Parent, and Lead.* Avery, 2015.

Burns, David D. *Feeling Good: The New Mood Therapy.* Harper, 2009.

Hendricks, Gay. *The Big Leap: Conquer Your Hidden Fear and Take Life to the Next Level.* HarperCollins, 2010.

Watts, Alan. The Book on the Taboo Against Knowing Who You Are. Souvenir Press, 2012.

Race

Baldwin, James, and Raoul Peck. *I Am Not Your Negro: A Major Motion Picture Directed by Raoul Peck.* Vintage International, Vintage Books, a Division of Penguin Random House LLC, 2017.

Baldwin, James. *Oxford Collected Essays.* Literary Classics of the United States, 1998.

Byrd, Ayana D., and Akiba Solomon. *Naked: Black Women Bare All about Their Skin, Hair, Hips, Lips, and Other Parts.* Berkley Pub. Group, 2005.

Collins, Patricia Hill. *Black Sexual Politics: African Americans, Gender, and the New Racism.* Routledge, 2006.

Lorde, Audre. *Sister Outsider: Essays and Speeches.* Crossing Press, 2015.

Moraga, Cherríe, and Gloria Anzaldúa. *This Bridge Called My Back Writings by Radical Women of Color.* SUNY Press, 2015.

Owens, Lama Rod., and Angel Kyodo Williams. *Radical Dharma.* North Atlantic Books, U.S., 2016

Sonja Renee Taylor - Founder of The Body is Not an Apology, a digital media and education company promoting radical self-love and body empowerment
SonyaReneeTaylor.com

The Mash-up Americans Podcast

MashupAmericans.com

Other: Mixed Race in America Podcast
WashingtonPost.com

Code Switch Podcast
NPR.org

TED (Technology, Entertainment and Design)
Ideas Worth Spreading – Curated talks on the
topic of Race.
TED.com/topics/race

National Hispanic Media Coalition **NHMC.org**

Sexuality and Sexual Trauma

Layla Martin - A great resource for all things sex,
including how to help your partner work with
you as trauma is triggered in bed
Layla-Martin.com

Saida Desilets - To learn about how the ancient
practices of the jade egg can heal your trauma
and delve into teachings about living fully in your
erotic genius.
SaidaDesilets.com

Leonore Tjia – Luminous Sex helps people understand the parts of themselves that cause inner conflict, and bring a beautiful, non-pathologizing method of understanding human problems and the complex world of sexuality. **LeonoreTjia.com**

Louise Mazanti -expert in sex, intimacy and consciousness and works in conjunction with her partner Mike Lousada **MazantLlousada.com**

Mike Lousada - provides both psychosexual somatic work that combines neuroscience, trauma therapy, myofacial release technique, psychotherapy and bodywork. He covers a wide range of sexual issues including trauma related to less touched on topics such as childbirth, miscarriage, etc. **MikeLousada.com**

Patti Britton - a clinical sexologists with a wide array of sex oriented support. **DrPattiBritton.com**

Eva Louise Williams - provides sacred feminine yoga and somatic bodywork for women including trauma release. **EvaLouiseWilliams.com**

Somatic Experiencing and how it can help heal trauma. **Traumahealing.org**

Diego Walraff - certified sexologist providing workshops and retreats in the area of sexual healing, tantra and intimacy.
ATouchFromTheHeart.com

Willow Brown - Taoist sexuality instructor and works in the area of women's health
YinWellness.com

Jennica Mills - works with the sexual assault recovery and facilitates healing through Neurogenic Yoga, TRE, and intuitive healing sessions.
Neurogenic-yoga.squarespace.com

Connie Eberhart - combines yoga in her healing work and provides both sexual wellness, pelvic health and other support.
Sacredembodiment.net

Peter Levine - groundbreaking audio exercises to heal sexual trauma. He has many other books and resources on this topic. *Sexual Healing: Transforming the Sacred Wound (Transform the Sacred Wound)*

Dalychia Saah and Rafaella Fiallo / Afrosexology - birthed out of a desire to experience a more sex-positive Black community. Visit their resources page for more reading on sexuality and race.
Afrosexology.com

Ardea, Naomi. *The Art of Healing from Sexual Trauma Tending Body and Soul Through Creativity, Nature, and Intuition.* Wise Ink, 2016.

Bessel Van der Kolk Bessel. *The Body Keeps the Score: Brain, Mind, and Body in the Healing of Trauma.* Penguin Books, 2015.

Byrd, Ayana D., and Akiba Solomon. *Naked: Black Women Bare All about Their Skin, Hair, Hips, Lips, and Other Parts.* Berkley Pub. Group, 2005.

Women

Bolen, Jean Shinoda. *Goddesses in Everywoman: Powerful Archetypes in Women's Lives; Gods in Everyman: Archetypes That Shape Men's Lives.* One Spirit, 2003.
Orenstein, Peggy. *Cinderella Ate My Daughter: Dispatches from the Front Lines of the New Girlie-Girl Culture.* Harper, 2012.

Simmer-Brown, Judith. Dakini's *Warm Breath: The Feminine Principle in Tibetan Buddhism.* Shambhala, 2003.

Simmons, Rachel. *The Curse of the Good Girl: Raising Authentic Girls with Courage and Confidence.* Penguin Books, 2010.

Hains, Rebecca. *Why Disney princesses and 'princess culture' are bad for girls.* Washington Post, June 24, 2016.

MissRepresentation - inspires individuals and communities to challenge and overcome limiting stereotypes so that everyone – regardless of gender, race, class, age, religion, sexual orientation, ability, or circumstance – can fulfill their human potential.
The RepresentationProject.org

See Jane - founded by Geena Davis, working within the media and entertainment industry to engage, educate, and influence content creators, marketers and audiences about the importance of eliminating unconscious bias in entertainment and media
SeeJane.org

The Harvard Women and Public Policy Program - closes gender gaps in economic opportunity, political participation, health and education by creating knowledge, training leaders and informing public policy and organizational practices.
Wappp.hks.harvard.edu

Lauren Paul and Molly Thompson – founded a non-profit organization to bring awareness and healing to the lasting pain of girl-against-girl bullying
KindCampaign.com

Tabby Biddle – an advocate for women's voices and feminine thought leadership
TabbyBiddle.com

TED (Technology, Entertainment and Design) Ideas Worth Spreading – Curated talks on the subject of women by TED speakers all over the world.
TED.com/topics/women

Women's Media Center
WomensMediaCenter.com

Made in the USA
Las Vegas, NV
18 March 2022

45909118R00173